Without Sympathy or Enthusiasm

Victor A. Thompson

Without Sympathy or Enthusiasm

The Problem of Administrative Compassion

The University of Alabama Press

University, Alabama

Contents

1

The Problem Defined

Mary Brown didn't mind that her husband, Laurence, an Air
Force sergeant, was being sent to Vietnam. Only she wanted to
be with him. To that end, the Air Force nurse, a lieutenant, extended her service for 15 months with, she claims, a promise they
would serve at the same base. On Friday the Danvers (Mass.)
couple said he got orders for Phan Rang. She's assigned to Ton
Son Nhut, 160 miles away. "I feel I was deliberately deceived to
make me re-enlist," she said.[1]

Aside from its "human interest" aspect, this story raises a fundamental question about organizations: Can an institution make personal promises? Stories such as this abound. They make good newspaper copy. Every reader sympathizes with the couple; the story
reinforces his low evaluation of bureaucracy, possibly paralleling an
experience of his own.

This kind of story stimulated the most widely distributed and
deeply held sociological theory of bureaucracy, the notion that
bureaucrats invest the means of administration with more value
than they do the ends—the "inversion of means and ends," or
"the displacement of goals." In fact, a leading book on organization comes close to stating that this proposition *is* the sociological
theory of bureaucracy.[2] Administration has been defined as the tri-
umph of technique over purpose.

Although the proposition antedates Robert Merton's famous
essay on "Bureaucratic Structure and Personality," published in

1940, he, too, uses such a story to launch his discussion of the inversion of means and ends.[3] He quotes a story from the *Chicago Tribune* concerning Bernt Balchen, Admiral Byrd's pilot in the flight over the South Pole.

> According to a ruling of the department of labor, Bernt Balchen . . . cannot receive his citizenship papers. Balchen, a native of Norway, declared his intention in 1927. It is held that he has failed to meet the condition of five years' continuous residence in the United States. The Byrd antarctic voyage took him out of the country, although he was on a ship carrying the American flag, was an invaluable member of an American expedition, and in a region to which there is an American claim because of the exploration and occupation of it by Americans, this region being Little America.
>
> The bureau of naturalization explains that it cannot proceed on the assumption that Little America is American soil. That would be *trespass on international questions* where it has no sanction. So far as the bureau is concerned, Balchen was out of the country and technically has not complied with the law of naturalization.[4]

In this case, the special circumstances of Bernt Balchen were not recognized. He was treated universalistically as one instance of a special problem category, not as a unique individual. If I had been making these decisions, I am sure that I would have given Mr. Balchen his citizenship and sent the nurse to live with her husband. I suspect that I would have reacted to the unique and personal aspects of these cases. But can modern organizations respond in that way?[5]

A few years ago I read a short item in a Gary, Indiana, newspaper that captured the essence of this problem. A state trooper had stopped a car that was driving down a country road at night without lights and weaving slowly back and forth across the road. The driver had no license. A woman was in the passenger side of the front seat. A man and a woman occupied the back seat. They were taken in and a ticket was issued and bond posted. Very simple. There was more information, however, that was irrelevant to the administrative problem and its disposition. A police reporter wrote up the whole case, including the additional, but administratively irrelevant, information. It seems the man driving the car had been blind from birth and had never experienced the feeling of driving a car. His wife and some friends decided to take him out on a quiet moonlit night on a quiet stretch of road and let him drive for a few minutes. The lights were not on because he did not need them. Of course, he had no driver's license. The car was weaving for obvious reasons. But all of these facts were irrelevant to the problem category that he represented to the police. Once this category had been established, the associated routines rolled out of the mill as inevitably as time.[6] Could it have been different? Could the local organization have acted compassionately? That is the question I have set out to answer in this little book.

Stories like the above are commonplace. They make good newspaper copy. Most people can identify with the client in such cases because most people have acquired certain emotional habits and needs by being brought up in the small group security of the nuclear family. They want to be treated as special cases. They want someone to "really care." They do not want to be just problem categories. They want compassion.

Many of the frustrations of individuals when dealing with the large organization arise from the scope of the particular problem or transaction they attempt to negotiate. The typical problem or transaction of an organization is too large for effective handling by an individual, given the current technology (e.g., that involved in making an automobile). Otherwise, it would be very difficult to explain the existence of organizations. Furthermore, given this broad scope, the range of persons interested in the outcome of the transaction is normally much broader than the individual client, and these broader interests usually have some kind of organizational representation, governmental or private. The effects of this situation on the gratifications or frustrations of the individual client, and on the individual organization employee, have been clearly stated elsewhere:

> Administrative action in the modern world is impersonal and institutional. It is not the product of one person's mind or heart. It reflects the concerns of all legitimate interests in the appropriate administrative constituency. Elaborate horizontal clearances and coordinating procedures assure this broad scanning of proposals before action. Furthermore, administrative action is expected to

be (and usually is) objective, impersonal, unsentimental, occasioned by universalistic criteria rather than particularistic personal appeals or sympathies. To protect against charges of subjectivity or personal favoritism, considerable documentation is collected before any action is taken. All of this preparation takes time and frequently leads to charges of bureaucratic red tape.

This impersonal, objective, institutional approach to action, while demanded by the norms of an industrial society, is somewhat at war with basic sociopsychological needs of individuals, most of whom have been socialized in primary groups where personal loyalty and action are stressed. Clienteles press for particularistic treatment, and many are tempted to use primary relations with officials to secure it. Reciprocally, officials may be tempted to appropriate authority to their personal use so that such particularistic requests can be granted (or denied). The desire for money side-payments need not be behind this conversion of institutional power to personal use. In fact, in the modern age it is probably more likely to be the understandable human need to be rewarded with gratitude or admiration.

Consequently, administrative assurances are sometimes given which cannot subsequently be redeemed. They cannot be passed through the impersonal, objective, institutionalized decision-making process of the bureaucracy. Generally speaking, if an individual has the personal power to grant or withhold favors, he has managed to appropriate administrative power to his personal use. One of the hardest lessons modern industrialized man has had to learn is neither to demand nor to promise special favors.[7]

Often, however, the problem presented or the transaction attempted by the individual client is too small for the organization and it is left to an individual functionary to give an appropriate explanation of an event, to write an appropriate letter, to carry out a simple restitutive routine (such as exchanging a returned item for another from stock), or to initiate an appropriate and simple automatic routine of the organization (such as giving credit for a returned item). Some of the most frustrating client experiences develop out of such small-scope problem situations. The employee may misunderstand the nature of the problem, either because of poor communication on the part of the client or, on the part of the functionary, a low capacity for understanding (being "not very bright"), an inadequate rehearsal of organization routines because of newness in the role, or unfortunate attitudinal postures of indifference or even hostility (such as that arising from racial prejudice or a client gesture interpreted as threatening).

A colleague of mine experienced a typical case of this kind. Upon moving into a new house, he had gotten an estimate from a local firm for the cost of attaching some electrical appliances. When the bill came, it was more than the estimate. He refused to pay it. Several letters and telephone calls (and months) later, he received a check for the difference between the estimate and the bill—which he had not paid. He finally decided that the easiest way out would be simply to pay the inflated bill. His work took him to many underdeveloped countries where experiences of this kind are common. As he said, "I decided that if they wanted to do it the hard way, it was all right with me." He regarded the whole situation as comic rather than infuriating and frustrating. By virtue of his travels, he was accustomed to such situations.

Another colleague tells of recently trying to pay a motel bill somewhere in the West. The clerk asked him for his credit cards. He said he did not use them; he would pay cash. She had no instructions covering so outlandish a situation and had to call her supervisor—but not before he had given her a short lecture on the theory of money. He was an economist.

Mass industrial society poses many challenges to individuals. The resulting malaise is too complex to be easily understood, but one has to be deaf not to hear the cry for compassionate treatment, as witness the phenomenal growth of "hotlines"—telephone numbers that troubled individuals can call to get friendly advice or help on problems from lost dogs to drugs to suicide. A generation ago it was speculated that perhaps at the bottom of much industrial conflict was an alienated, lonesome, frightened, insecure working man who wanted his company to respond to him warmly and personally. He could not strike for love; so he sublimated his need into a demand, through his union, for better wages and hours.

If this depiction of the industrial worker has some merit, how many more persons must be in this fix today. Not just industrial laborers, but white collar functionaries, students, clients of large government agencies, customers of the giant private companies— all of us at times receive and hate the dehumanizing, stripping treatment dealt out by mass administration, from having our identity turned into a number (usually the Social Security number) to having our brief cases searched when we leave the library. Part of the recent program of campus activism was aimed at this dehumanization. Activists harangued the students: "They don't care about you."

Suggestions of all kinds, such as academic proposals for a "new political science" or a "new public administration," are stimulated in part by a strong need to bring compassion into our affairs. Someone has to care.[8] Internation dealing will often turn on popular evaluation of the compassion in the arrangements. States are personified in the persons of their leaders and in this way abstract reality is rendered intimate, personal, understandable, compassionate. Media evaluation of events is largely of this kind, the important question being the motives of the actors—their kindness, honesty, altruism, sincerity, compassion. A good example is a late-1971 column about former President Richard M. Nixon ("Unpredictable Nixon") by James Reston that he ended in this way: "And this is where we are at the beginning of the new year—or so it seems here—alive, but confused and divided. And the paradox of it is that the new year is a presidential election year, and the central issue of the election may very well be between the men who are clever and the men who can be trusted." Counterculture religions are proliferating to cater to the needs of people (mostly young) seeking identity and companionship in an impersonal world. Such religions are often substitutes for the more extreme adaptations of drugs (for which, indeed, they are often cures).

Rightly or wrongly, industrial societies increasingly channel the energies of their members through the large, purposive, rationalized organizations that we have come to call bureaucracies. Not only productive or economic energies but much expressive energy is likewise so channeled, as in organized religion, organized sports, administered vacations, highly regulated parks and forests and campsites, and in many other areas of life. For many students, modernity is equated with organizations. Modern society has been called the "organizational society," modern man the "organization man."[9]

The organization of minorities into neighborhood corporations or various kinds of action groups, like the organization of workers into unions, concerns a different problem. These are political events aimed at concentrating power with the idea of affecting policies. I am discussing the problem of the individual in the application of policies, and that problem, as I shall seek to demonstrate in the chapters that follow, remains the same regardless of the policy.

2

The Nature of
Modern Organizations

Can modern organizations be compassionate? Can they "care"? Can organizations be depicted as good or bad, kind or cruel? From everything we know about modern organizations, the answer has to be "No!" In this essay I want to explore briefly why this has to be the answer, why the need for compassion persists, and what kinds of adaptations or solutions to this serious impasse have occurred or been suggested. If I succeed in clarifying the situation, perhaps more human ingenuity will be spent in seeking imaginative solutions and less in empty rhetoric and despairing cries of anguish.

There are two sides to the problem. On the one side is the organization and its nature, on the other, the individual person and his needs. Let me discuss the nature of the organization first. The key to both the number and nature of modern organizations is specialization, or "differentiation" as the sociologists say. Even as individuals specialize in function or occupation to survive competitively in the face of explosively increasing knowledge and technique, organizations specialize or differentiate to channel these specialized skills to meet needs of specialized customers, clients, or interested groups. Fewer and fewer needs can be met by individual efforts, and this state of affairs generates the need for more and more organizations.[1]

These organizations are staffed, increasingly, by specialists who deal not with human beings but with categories of problems. They deal with one kind of problem affecting many people rather than with many kinds of problems affecting few people. Specialists are psychologically incapable of becoming personally and deeply involved with all these people. Furthermore, only a small amount of information about the customer, or client, or colleague is relevant to the solution of the specialized problem. The client becomes part of a problem category, not a historical person: he becomes an applicant for welfare, a speeder, a cardiac case, etc. In this transaction, he is not a person. The transaction is impersonal, and this fact actually facilitates the expert solution of his problem. Interpersonal emotions do not interfere with the instrumental application of the specialist's expertise. ("He who is his own lawyer has a fool for a client," as the lawyers say.) But the client suffers the absence of compassion— he is not important just because he is he; his treatment is contingent. Payment of the fee is only one of the contingencies. His unique individuality, which is his identity, is ignored.[2]

In past times, with low mobility and very stable social relations, it was not always easy to separate the person from what he did day in and day out. The distinction between person and role was difficult to make. People became what they did and many modern names have come down to us from this period: Mason, Smith, Carpenter, Schumaker, etc.

An enormous increase in mobility, first geographic, then social, and finally psychological, has made the distinction between person and role easier for us to make. People can choose roles as they choose merchandise. As Max Weber said, one of the criteria of modern organization ("bureaucracy") is the separation of person and office, of personal rights and public rights, of person and role.[3] With this modern discriminatory skill, it becomes possible to think of fashioning or designing organizations for achieving specific purposes just as we design physical tools or instruments for achieving certain purposes. Recognizing the organization as a designed tool or instrument adds several dimensions to our problem of administrative compassion.

There are at least two basic roles in tool construction.[4] There is, of course, the "designer," an engineer with knowledge of the means to the accomplishment of various ends of other people. There is, too, the designer's client, the "person" who has a need for which a tool must be constructed. Let us call this role that of the "owner." The values that the tool is designed to achieve are "his." (I use quotes to indicate that these terms are usually personifications of much more abstract social entities.)

An organization-tool uses people rather than inanimate things such as motors, cogs, and belts. People have values, goals, preference orderings, just as owners do. These values must be neutralized or else what is finally designed will be anything but a tool; whatever it might be would pull and haul in all directions, and its "accomplishments" would only be predictable, if at all, by systems analysis. It would have outcomes rather than outputs.

To avoid this result, to actually construct an organization-tool, an additional role is needed—that of "functionary." A functionary does his duty, applies his skills, performs his practiced routines, regardless of what goal or whose goal is involved.[5] A screwdriver does not choose among goals or among owners. It does what it is "told." To induce individual persons to enter or perform the functionary role, designers and owners enter into an exchange contract with them, the employment contract. In return for sufficient values, such as salaries, prestige, power, and a chance at increasing one or more of these, the employee gives up his own values or uses for the organization in deference to those of the owner, thereby leaving a single, consistent, ordering of values by virtue of which all behavior of functionaries can be coordinated and the relative success or failure of the organization-tool assessed. In public organizations we often use the term "servant" instead of or in addition to "functionary." The owner of the public organization in the modern period is, of course, "the people" (it used to be a feudal king).

As noted above, the test of the organizational tool, the criterion by which it is judged, kept, abolished, or modified, is external to the organization; it is the goal or preference ordering of the owner. There is no room for another test, such as the need of employees for "joy in work," or the need of clients for "compassion." We do not build tools to fight with themselves, to undo what they do. The goal of a public welfare organization, for example, is what the "public" wants for recipients of welfare, not what the welfare recipients want for themselves.

To recognize compassion in administration is to recognize another claim; it is to "steal" the owner's property. Today it is likely that such "theft" exists on a fairly large scale, since employees highly identified with "the poor" interpret their role to be that of agents of "the poor" within the welfare organization. They interpret their obligation to be to the client rather than to the owner, and they get all the money (or other goods) they possibly can for the client regardless of the plans and intentions (regulations) of the owners. The extent of this kind of behavior has not been measured but it has probably contributed to the astronomical rise in welfare costs.[6] Other interest groups have long tried (and often successfully) to get *their* "agents" strategically located in bureaucratic organizations so that they could appropriate the owner's values, witness the federal departments of labor, commerce, and agriculture.

A recent meeting of young teachers of public administration defined what they were pleased to call the "new public administration."[7] Employees (officials, functionaries) are to use their special resources to take from those who have money and power and give to those who have not, regardless of the goals of the "owner," like a company of modern Robin Hoods. The "new public administration" is a call for equality by means of "theft" and "subversion" on the basis of the ageless fallacy that the end justifies the means.[8]

It is true that if an administrative official could in some way appropriate various administrative resources (money, jobs, authority, etc.) to his own use, he could then use them as he personally wanted, within the remaining organizational limits that he could not control. He could even use such appropriated resources to afford compassionate treatment, if he so wanted. Such a use of personally appropriated resources would almost certainly be selective—or, as social scientists say, particularistic rather than universalistic. Probably no one is indifferent as between the members of any possible pair of people. Our lucky administrator, who had appropriated resources so that he could grant or deny favors, say yes or no at will, would undoubtedly bestow his favors, his "compassion," according to whom the would-be beneficiary was, rather than solely according to the merits of the claim. Some would bestow the favor only for a monetary price ("corruption," in the modern world). It is difficult to see how sane persons could seriously advocate the personal appropriation of administrative resources by administrators as a solution to the problem of compassion.[9]

Such theft of resources nevertheless takes place, though in less obvious ways than it did in the preindustrial past and still does in the underdeveloped countries. In the past,[10] office frequently became private property, to buy, sell, or inherit. In the past, it was a frequent device to have the expenses of an office, including the officeholder's salary, financed from his fees or other collections from clients ("prebendary financing"). We still find this pattern in some local-government areas in this country (as, for instance, in some justice-of-the-peace jurisdictions). In the past, and even now in most underdeveloped countries, it was and is customary for officeholders to use their resources in such a way as to give preference to friends, kinsmen, and (later) fellow political-party members. In some parts of the world today, it is customary to "purchase" favorable administrative action through the payment of "*baksheesh*," or as we would say, bribes or kickbacks. In many places, such as in Mexico, it is customary to hire a professional intermediary to solicit preferential treatment for oneself, a person we would call a "five percenter."[11]

While all these older forms of individual appropriation of administrative resources still exist in modern society to a certain extent, they conflict with modern administrative morality and so are considerably reduced. Newer or simply more subtle forms, however, have taken their place. Resources are unevenly distributed as symbols of rank or status: office size, furniture, rugs, parking places, company cars and drivers, etc. More important than the personal use of resources as symbols of rank and as marks of deference is the effect of status rank on the distribution of influence, on the flow of information and communication, on the initiation of ideas and suggestions, on the correction of errors. Highly positioned individuals acquire personal power from the irrational distortions that arise from status rank. Within some limits, they can make arbitrary exceptions in the application of organization routines or changes therein. They can, therefore, dispense some personal ("compassionate") treatment. Control systems in organizations have never been perfectly efficient; they leave some leeway, some elbow room, in which to juggle budgets, to manipulate reports and budget requests, to edit the information available to higher authority.[12] To recognize administrative discretion, however, is a far cry from advocating the personal appropriation of administrative resources as a device for solving the problems of inequality, poverty, or any like problem.

The organization-tool is a consciously adopted design for goal accomplishment. It is a system, in the same fashion as an automobile is a system, in that all parts are related to all others by reference to their presumed relevance to a single set goal. It is an artificially contrived system. As such, it is a hundred percent prescription. It is a system of roles and rules. It does not describe behavior; it prescribes it. Though it has and must have motivational elements in it, they are encased in a prescriptive plan that is to be carried out by functionaries acting according to rules and roles in a very roundabout fashion. The rewards and penalties of the motivational plan are not direct; they are administered—they are mediated by functionaries. In the artificial system, all relationships are impersonal and abstract. There is not only no compassion; there is no way that compassion can be included. Compassion cannot be prescribed. The idea of a designed role of "administrator of compassion" is ludicrous.

Theoretically, compassionate employees could be selected. However, competence to achieve the "owner's" goal will seem more important, and in the likely case of conflict between goal and compassion, only one choice is possible; compassion must go unless it indeed *is* the goal. Again, the design may meet public relations needs by special training in compassion for people in boundary roles such as counter clerk. But this is difficult to bring off. To sensitive clients, synthetic compassion can seem worse than none at all. In the final analysis, compassion is an individual gift, not an organizational one.

Much has been made of the distinction between functional and substantive rationality, the first being the rational application of means to prescribed ends, while the second is defined as the evaluation ("rationality") of the ends themselves. The distinction is illustrated in the humorous epigram that used to circulate in Washington: What is not worth doing at all is not worth doing well. Starting with Max Weber and Karl Mannheim, it has been fashionable to argue that working in a government organization (and now business organizations, as well)—that is, being a bureaucrat, a functionary—affects the mind so that one can only be functionally rational. Generally, no explanation of this transformation is given.

14

Robert Merton tried to explain it as the effect of bureaucratic structure on personality.[13]

Apart from the question of whether it is appropriate to apply the norm of rationality to the evaluation of goals,[14] these sociological formulations are not convincing. In the first place, they are reductionistic attempts to explain sociological phenomena in terms of psychological variables. Furthermore, if bureaucracy is so easily criticized, why has it not changed? There must be more to it. If bureaucrats (functionaries) claimed the right to set or alter goals, not only democracy but all other kinds of government (and industry) would be impossible. Besides, these imputed intellectual cripples, the bureaucrats, have agreed explicitly or implicitly to confine their expertise, their functional rationality, to the achievement of the "owner's" goals. They are under a contractual (as well as a more general moral) obligation to do so. Were this not so, every participant in the organization would have a *liberum veto* over all collective action.

Strangely enough, functionaries (bureaucrats) are accused both of lacking substantive rationality and of usurping the political function by exercising too great an influence over goals.[15] For many students of administration the number one problem is how to suppress the substantive rationality of bureaucrats or, in other words, the problem of how to control them.[16] The central concern of organizational design and of management is control, and control ultimately means control of the functionaries.

The doctrine of functional versus substantive rationality is part of the antiestablishment bias that has characterized much of sociology almost from the beginning.[17] Functionaries apply their expertise disproportionately to the means because that is what our institutions expect them to do and because the reward/penalty procedures of our organizations are designed to secure this orientation. There is no mystery here, nor any grounds for criticism of functionaries. "They have a job to do."

The sociological attack on functionaries, well illustrated by that of William Howton, amounts to the personification of a role. Most of us play functionary roles of some kind, at some time, in some organization. The incumbent of the role is just a person, concerned with ends as much as means, concerned with problems of life, and just as capable of rendering personal evaluations of ultimate ends as sociologists are. In the final analysis, what *is* the "substantive rationality" of sociology? The prejudices of sociologists? Was General Lavelle being substantively rational when he bombed North Vietnam contrary to orders from higher authority? Does the reader agree that he was rightly fired for doing so?

Organization-tools are different from others in that the materials of which they are composed are autonomous, goal-forming creatures. They are human beings. As such, they have the need to preserve themselves, their values, and their self-images—they have survival needs. They also have the propensity to interact and thereby to spontaneously generate roles and behavior norms and to enforce them informally upon one another. They have a strong tendency to become interlocked in an unplanned, spontaneous system. Considering that it is spontaneous, unplanned, and without a goal, let us call this system the "natural system" of the organization. Since this system arises without the roles of designer and owner, there is no external criterion to which it is beholden. Its only criterion is internal. As for all other natural systems, this criterion is survival.

The natural system of informal norms and roles grows up spontaneously to protect the survival needs of the incumbents of the functionary roles. Survival-endangering behavior, such as competition, high individual production, and the rate and direction of change, are informally brought under control, to the extent possible. Endangering personal obligations such as responsibility or risk are informally reduced or spread around in some way, if this is possible. To accomplish their "mission," natural systems, if allowed to do so, reach states of equilibrium and develop homeostatic processes to reduce deviating swings from these states and to restore them by counterswings, if possible. The form of the process is much like the negative feedback of a thermostatically controlled heating system. Duplicating methods and capabilities develop informally to reduce the risk of failure with its associated threat to the individual. Strangely enough, many formally important organizational functions, such as innovation, structural flexibility, and much of the motivating, are performed in this unplanned, spontaneous system.

Natural systems do not have decision-making organs and hence cannot be studied by the methods of logical or policy analysis. They are studied by statistically controlled empirical observation. Because a society is a natural system (a prime example of one, in fact), moral evaluations of a society—calling it "irrational," "racist," etc.—are either senseless or a form of poetic license. So, too, is the rather common practice of blaming society for various individual failures. Artificial systems, however, such as governments, do have decision-making organs—legislatures, administrative agencies, constitutional conventions—to which evaluative terms of various kinds, rational or moral, are properly applied. They act; they make choices. They have outputs, whereas natural systems, such as societies, have outcomes. To blame a natural system for anything makes no more sense than to blame nature, also a natural system, or a subsystem of nature such as gravity.

Natural systems are not established. Given the appropriate conditions, they develop. The appropriate conditions seem to be occasions and time for stable interactions. Organizations whose technologies and products are stable undergo such natural systemic development that they become almost impervious to change. Schools are a good example of this process.[18] On the other hand, in organizations that use a dynamic and changing technology, the equilibria and homeostatic processes of natural systems are never fully developed. Such organizations are much easier to change by their designers and owners.

The natural system of an organization, because it develops in response to artificial-system demands and responsibilities, becomes in time a unified system rather than a collection of small natural systems or groups. The artificial system is "monocratic"; it is unified by reference to the owner's goal (which may, of course, be a system or set of consistent goals). What unity the organizational natural system acquires depends upon its derivative nature. It derives from a unified artificial system.

This essay is not the place for further discussion of natural-systems development in organizations or the conditions that facilitate or retard this development. One point, however, must be made. There is a potential conflict between the owner's interest and the natural system—between "cost-benefit analysis" of goal accomplishment and survival needs. This potential conflict raises control to the principal position in all artificial-system processes. Control attempts to assure a reasonable meeting of the external criterion, attainment of the owner's goals. Meeting this test is one, and usually the principal, condition for survival of the natural system.

Whatever else a modern public (or private) organization is, therefore, it is a machinelike instrument or tool of an external power. It is an artificial system of prescribed roles and rules. It is not a person. It is not a parent or friend. It is an abstract system of interrelationships designed to achieve an externally defined goal. Roles are bundles of duties (and powers). They do not care; they have no feelings. Whereas a particular incumbent of a role may "care" for a particular client (or customer, etc.), the caring is not part of the organizational plan. In fact, such a caring relation between the incumbent of a role in a modern organization and a client is regarded as unethical, as giving the client "pull," perhaps in the form of nepotism or favoritism.

We are proud of the fact that modern administration, as compared with administration in the past, is relatively free of such "particularistic" behavior and is "universalistic," instead.[19] We are proud of the fact that modern administration gives jobs to people who merit them rather than to people who need them. Departures from such impersonal (noncompassionate) performance are pounced upon by the media; the departures make good news stories precisely because they violate modern canons of good administration. Why should a modern role incumbent care about a client? Who cares for *him*, other than his family and close friends? He, too, is caught up in an abstract, impersonal network, the artificial system, the organization-tool.[20]

Furthermore, constructing organizations of abstract, impersonal roles eliminates (though not entirely) the relevance of the personal relations between role incumbents, whether they be love, hate, or indifference. The officially prescribed relationships exclude this aspect of interpersonal relations. Otherwise each organization would be unique, like a family, very few organizations would exist, and this country could support no more people than it did in 1492, perhaps about 800,000. The exclusion of personal elements from prescribed role relations has made the modern organization possible and adequate to its logistical task of provisioning hundreds of millions of people.

Most people in economically and politically underdeveloped countries cannot understand an abstract administrative order. Their relationships are personal, their obligations are personal, and they are unable to fashion organization-tools. That is why they are underdeveloped.[21] For lack of organizations, their political actions, obligations, and interests are personal—"compassionate." There is no "public" interest. There is no "owner" of the public organization, the accomplishment of whose goal is the test of said organization. Everyone simply gets all he can get. Compassion monopolizes administration.

Still the problem of administrative compassion remains. Most people are brought up in a small intimate group, the so-called nuclear family. Their earliest and most constant experiences involve emotional dependence and support—involve, that is, compassion. In a thousand ways, we come to need such treatment, to be treated as whole and unique individuals whose feelings are important. We do not experience ourselves as "problem categories." We learn to expect incredible amounts of effort to be expended on our behalf, just because of our feelings. ("We forgot the Teddy Bear. We'll have to drive back [100 miles] and get it.") We do not want to have to justify ourselves, to live with contingency.

We are modern men and women. We believe in the principle of equality before the law, we believe in "universalistic" norms of administration, and yet we are ambivalent. We want administration to be universalistic (noncompassionate) in general, but how could making a little exception in our case hurt anything, an exception that would have no perceptible effect on public administration but would do a tremendous amount of good for us?

Our first experience of the large, abstract, impersonal organization can be devastating. For many young people this first experience is college. Yet how much worse it would be for a person brought up in the extended family or clan of traditional society! It is said that there once existed a tribe (in New Zealand, I believe) that punished serious infractions of social norms by treating the culprit as a nonperson. Everyone acted as if he were not there—a sort of social banishment. People so treated, it is said, died in about three months, on the average.[22]

Yes, the problem remains. The family has shrunk but it has not disappeared, and it is hard to imagine a viable alternative to it that would eliminate small-group experiences completely.[23] The modern organization, by its nature, can offer only impersonal, categorized, noncompassionate treatment. But many individuals apparently still need personalized, individualized, compassionate treatment by the ever more ubiquitous organization. What are some of the adaptations that occur in attempting to resolve this impasse?

3 SOLUTIONS

Personnel Administration

Administrative "compassion" can be thought of as special treatment, as "stretching" the rules, as the premodern "rule of men" rather than the "rule of law." In the modern period such behavior is denigrated in such terms as "amicism" ("pull" from highly placed friends or relatives), nepotism, and corruption (purchased compassion). From early in our history, faithful party service bought one compassion ("spoils"). While such behavior will continue so long as people feel the need for compassionate, individualized treatment, it can hardly be suggested as a solution of our problem. What else, then?

An adaptation obvious enough to have occurred to almost everyone is simply to staff administrative agencies with compassionate personnel. A characteristic phenomenon of the times is the appearance of organizations whose purpose is to aid those who feel that they do not get satisfaction from the more established institutions of our society: clinics staffed by young idealistic medical personnel who work for little (relatively) or nothing, storefront law firms staffed by young, idealistic legal personnel who charge low (or even no) fees. In the first blush of enthusiasm for this approach, even some governmental organizations appeared (such as legal aid under the Office of Economic Opportunity), but the power-redistribution implications of these activities were soon recognized and they were put under harness or abolished.

The storefront, young-idealist approach is pathetically inadequate because there are not enough competent young idealists around even to make a meaningful beginning, and besides, most of those who go into this kind of work continue in it for only a short time; the powerful pull of a promise of large incomes, reinforced by the absence of gratitude, soon wrestles the idealist conscience to uncomfortable silence. Those who would be benefactors must be prepared to be hated by the beneficiaries of their good deeds—by those whose own inadequacies are so painfully pointed out.[1] The phenomenon is probably a passing fad, and, in any event, provides staff only for small antiestablishment establishments, not the giant bureaus in which most of the decisions governing us are made.

An exception to the above is the nursing profession, which selects a large proportion of people who have strong needs to help others and provides a training that legitimizes and reinforces those needs. The hospital, therefore, probably comes the closest to being a compassionate organization, a fact that in itself underlines the extent of the problem.[2]

An older but basically similar approach—that is, an approach through personnel administration—is to give special attention to the problem in training those who "meet the public": counter clerks, bus drivers, etc. (I do not refer here to "T-Group" training, which is a basically different matter and which is discussed in the next chapter.) Although the training of counter clerks and others goes on continuously, it does not seem to solve the problem. One's friendly attitude towards one's fellow man is hardly a result of an administrative training program. Such buffer roles between frustrated and frightened clientele and a basically impersonal (hostile?) and abstract organization—an organization that controls employees' behavior in a roundabout fashion by means of rules and roles performed by functionaries—are not feasible on a large scale. The self-protection of the role incumbents often requires a hostile, or at best disinterested, treatment of the clientele, and the special training is soon forgotten.

Why should we expect it to be otherwise? When the young instructor, for example, wants his school to treat him with compassion, to treat him as his father used to do, just what is it that he wants? The school is not a person; it has no feelings. He wants his chairman to give him compassion, to show personal appreciation and recognition. But how about the personal problems of the chairman? Who will meet his needs for compassionate treatment? Who will stand *in loco parentis* to him? The dean? But the problem is still there. It cannot be generally solved because the organization, in the final analysis, has no feelings but operates through rules, and through roles filled by people who, on the average, have the same needs for compassion as the aforesaid young instructor.

Occasionally there is an exception to this general rule. An unusually "heroic" person gets into this chain of personification of the abstract—a person who is able to dispense compassionate behavior without receiving it himself. But one suspects that, as usual, the emotional costs must be paid somehow—in ulcers, in a beastly home life, in the ruined personalities of the "hero's" children.

Psychologists are especially prone to overlook this problem and to expect heroic persons to show up at the right time and place and in the right numbers. Thus, they write books on child psychology, when the problem is the psychology of the parents. Or they write books on the psychology of employees, suggesting managerial strategies for dealing with them more effectively, when a large part of the problem is the psychology of people who need to get into authority (manager) roles and succeed in doing so because they have enough *power* to make their psychology an important question. A sadist on the assembly line might spoil a few parts. A sadist in an authority role——?

Beyond these sufficient obstacles to solving the compassion problem through personnel administration (that is, the selection, training, and placement of personnel), there are other equally insurmountable obstacles to its success. Synthetic compassion can probably be detected by most people, and it has a stomach-turning quality. It makes the frustration, loneliness, fear, and alienation all the worse for those who see through it. It reproduces a response similar to that aroused by TV commercials.

Besides, this synthetic compassion is usually dispensed by those who have no power anyway—those who meet and absorb the public's problems but lack the authority to do anything about them. The kindly reassurances of the counter clerk are hollow, nor should a sophisticated customer take out his frustration on such a role player. Most of us know it is not his (her) fault. She (he) is powerless. The real holders of power are shielded from us by layer upon layer of such buffers, and organizational decision making is largely processual rather than personal, anyway. Taking it out on the counter clerk affords only a momentary relief, and it probably aggravates the problem in the long run—especially if one's conscience forces one to return to apologize to the counter clerk (or bus driver, or policeman, or store clerk). On top of the frustrating (dare I say "stupid"?) treatment, an apology is exacted by one's own conscience!

Any approach to an organizational problem through the attitudinal selection or training of personnel reduces the flexibility and hence the value of the organization to the "owner."[3] It is, therefore, a high-cost approach and also, if done without the owner's knowledge and permission, a form of theft. Should the owner wish to change his goals or values, he will find the tool unresponsive. Unless he can simply fire everyone and immediately hire an efficient new staff, he will have lost resources.

Organization Development and Sensitivity Training

Since most of us are members of large bureaucratic organizations, concern for more personalized or compassionate treatment of individuals by organizations naturally extends to employees as well as to clientele (or customers, patients, etc.). Several social psychologists, beginning at least with Elton Mayo, have been working on this problem for years. Many of them consult with organization managements about changing organizations or their supervisory styles. These psychologists have begun to call their field "organization development," and for simplicity's sake I will lump their efforts and theories together under that title.[1]

Organization development seeks to change organizations. It is casual about the purpose and direction of change because it relies upon a natural-system, natural-law concept of the "healthy" organization. Warren Bennis, for example, equates "scientific management" with "organization health." The natural-system (i.e., natural-law) origin of the concept is clear. "It is now possible to postulate the criteria for organization health. These are based on a definition by Marie Jahoda, according to which a healthy personality '. . . actively masters his environment, shows a certain unit[y] of personality, and is able to perceive the world and himself correctly.' Let us take each of these elements and extrapolate it into organizational criteria."[2] Frequently, it is urged that healthy organizations will be more effective in achieving their goals, but the major emphasis of organization development is that the organization be a more healthful environment in which adults can work. These people gloss over the fact that an organization is a tool of an external power (its "owner").

In the healthy organization, all relations are supportive; many motivations are harnessed (besides money), and all work in the same direction; employees are members of tightly knit solidarity groups; high-standard group goals are set by group decisions; communication is full and frank, both as to facts and feelings, and flows easily without distortion in all appropriate directions (not just from the top down); dealings are not one-to-one, boss-to-man, but more in the nature of group confrontations; relations are collaborative rather than "win/lose" competitive.

A basic problem is the common acceptance of the organization's goal—the problem of social order. Most organization-development advocates implicitly adopt a Rousseau-like position. Man's natural state is one of harmony; but his institutions have perverted him. In the healthy organization, each person would see that his own best interest was served by making the organization succeed. Rensis Likert suggests an elaborate semimechanical device of overlapping groups so that many hierarchical superiors would be group leaders of several groups, this multiple group membership being assumed to be powerful enough to bring about organizational unity rather than just to dampen the conflict.

One gets the feeling that some organization-development practitioners do not mind sacrificing the owner's goal, so long as individual employees obtain a more healthful working atmosphere—a sort of subconscious subversion. More serious are some apparently faulty empirical assumptions of organization development. First, there is no reason to assume that individual goals, or solidarity-group goals, will be consistent with those of the external power, the owner.[3] With the calculations impeccable on both sides, individuals and organizations can arrive at contrary and possibly conflicting conclusions with perfect rationality. And, of course, irrational behavior is common enough and can always lead to conflict.

Second, the relationship between employee morale and high production of the owner's goals has not only not been proved but may, if it holds at all, hold only under specific cultural conditions and with a reversed causal order. A worker with a strongly internalized norm (duty) of high production will experience personal satisfaction from high output. The satisfaction results from the output, not the reverse.[4]

Finally, even if one does not regard (as I do) the concept of a "healthy organization" to be natural-law metaphysics, it is still possible, even likely, that different production goals and conditions will require different organization structures. The "healthy organization" will not be optimal under most conditions, and perhaps not under very many conditions. Somehow, the picture of a strongly identifying group of workers and their boss sitting around planning high group-production goals for latrine digging is ludicrous. Claims of success for organization development often involve Research and Development or similar groups (often groups of salesmen). In any case, the success stories are few, and we have no way of knowing whether organization development was responsible.

Organization development is based on a natural-system organization model. Natural-law notions evolve easily from such models. The organization, however, is also an artificial system, a tool of an external power. As such, it is evaluated from an external vantage point by reference to how efficiently it produces the externally imposed goal. An organization, being composed of self-directing and structure-creating creatures, also develops over time into a natural system, one organized around the artificial. The criterion of the natural system is survival, which is a necessary quality of such systems. Conflict between the externally imposed criteria of the artificial system and the survival criterion of the natural system is not only possible but—I am sure some clever person can show it to be—inevitable, sooner or later.[5]

Organization-development practitioners have developed a change instrument that has broader implications and so must be listed as another device to aid in the solution of our problem of administrative compassion in the modern world. I refer to "laboratory training" or T-Group training. The T-Group (Training-Group) was developed by organization-development practitioners to facilitate organization change.[6] A group of trainees is brought together under a most permissive and nonstructuring "leader" in the hope that they will begin to explore the possibilities of fuller interpersonal communication both as to facts and (especially) feelings.

It is hoped that the trainees will develop skills in "authentic" communication without exploitative reservations, including both giving and taking, that is, both talking and listening. A by-product would be a great deal of self-knowledge and self-acceptance and the expansion of empathy. The whole thing is referred to as the development of interpersonal skills. Training groups can be composed in different ways: the trainees from many organizations, or a group of fellow workers and their boss ("family groups"), or members from different parts of the same organization, groups of people at the same hierarchical level (peers) or from several levels, etc.

T-Group training is very difficult to evaluate, but a great deal of effort has been spent trying to do so. Not wholly unexpectedly, its advocates find measurable changes both in the trainees and in their organizations after they return.[7] If one takes the evaluation of non-advocates a different story emerges. There is no convincing evidence that organizations have been changed by means of such training, and no one has yet attempted to show that production and efficiency have been improved by it.[8] Occasionally, however, new problems for organizations have been generated by T-Group training (for example, mass resignations of trainees).[9] Participating individuals, on the other hand, may experience great personal value from the sessions (or the opposite: there have been suicides), just as they might from listening to a Sunday sermon or contemplating a beautiful painting. Some kinds of small measurable attitude changes are often found; how long they last is another matter, and is not known.

Despite the meagerness of these findings, T-Group methods have become a large business, one with large investments in the form of personal reputations. They have also been commercialized through "encounter groups" into a multimillion-dollar fad, but this should probably not be blamed on the original organization-development psychologists who were seeking a way to change organizations in the direction of organization health.

Although the evidence does not support the idea that T-Group training will help solve the administrative-compassion problem, the technique has by now become so widely publicized and oversold that it has acquired great political utility to administrators. For example, one of the "nonnegotiable demands" of some groups critical of a school system or a police department may be that the employees in question be required to take "sensitivity training" (another synonym for T-Group). By agreeing to this demand, the administrator can get the political "monkey" off his back, even though he may know that he is making a zero contribution to solving the underlying problem. (Of course, he may conscientiously believe in the efficacy of the "therapy." Why should *he* know any better?)

When such a political agreement has been reached, requiring sensitivity training for all personnel of the agency, we have witnessed one of the most profound invasions of personal rights that can currently take place in our society. Such requirements are in the same category as requiring personnel to go to church and be "converted." They are only a step removed from the compulsory incarceration of perfectly sane political dissidents in mental institutions, allegedly so widely practiced in the Soviet Union. And yet who speaks out on behalf of these teachers, policemen, etc.? Their unions? The American Civil Liberties Union? The National Education Association? Not so that you can notice it.

Efforts to heighten the affective or personal aspect of interfunctionary relations in modern organizations have a basic flaw. As I have said, the artificial system, or formal organization, is composed of rules and roles. The roles prescribe necessary functional relations but eliminate the personal or affective aspect. Since these personal factors of love or hate are irrelevant (almost), anyone with the needed technical skill can be placed in the role. People are largely interchangeable, making it easily possible to construct all the organizations we need.

As the natural or informal system develops, however, spontaneous, informal roles develop in which the affective, personal aspects of interpersonal relations is very high. Informal, natural systems develop a high level of affect.[10] Here, as in so many other ways, we find a natural conflict between the natural and the artificial systems. To illustrate, the obligations of the role of friend may be incompatible with the obligation of the role of boss. In fact, studies of the behaviors in small groups, including small working groups, can raise the question of how the abstract, impersonal, modern bureaucratic organization is possible at all. Why do the interpersonal obligations (friendship, for example) of the natural system not thoroughly sabotage the interpersonal organizational duties of the artificial system? I think the answer must be that modern socialization gives rise to interpersonal obligations that are less demanding than those of the preindustrial era—personal obligations that are compatible with the prescribed formal role obligations of modern organization design.

Friendship, under our conditions of mobility, is more superficial than it used to be. Friends are no longer expected to "give the shirt off their backs." We meet our new fellow employees in the morning, are on a first-name basis by midafternoon, and may be transferred the next morning. Modern man has many acquaintances but few friends. He is lonely even in a crowd.[11]

When one's friend and peer is elevated to the role of boss, one does not expect to receive special treatment from him; none would be asked, and indeed the friendship would probably be allowed to terminate quickly. In June, 1960, *Modern Office Procedures,* a trade journal, advised newly promoted bosses to "Break away gradually—Recognize the simple fact of office life that the higher you go, the fewer friends you'll have in the company." "Give your friends in the office every chance to break away from you," the article continues. "They know you can't remain part of the old gang."[12] Adventures across the impersonal, functional borders of the role are allowed ritually only at certain times, such as at the office Christmas party or the annual picnic.[13] This miniscule recognition of the problem seems to be enough for modern man.

If the affective, personal element in interrole relationships within administration is enlarged, through sensitivity training or otherwise, the equilibrium between the natural and artificial systems of modern organizations may be sufficiently disturbed to reduce our ability to form organizations. If organizations become systems of interpersonal relations, like families, the number we can successfully field may fall below our functional requirements; the society and economy may regress toward a preindustrial "tribalism." Tampering with organizations is also tampering with personalities and must be undertaken with the same care and understanding. The carelessness and casualness with which organizational advice is handed out reflects the general lack of confidence in the advice and its actual ineffectiveness.

There are other problems connected with the training of employees, whether they be supervisors or those who deal with clients.[14] Most training conducted by the organization itself seeks to strengthen employee knowledge of the prescriptions of the artificial system and to reinforce their authoritative nature. The rules and regulations are reviewed and high-level superiors give pep talks to indicate that the organization really wants them obeyed and wants all employees (functionaries) to be loyal to the "owner's" objectives. Organization-run training is usually of this kind because such training is part of the central concern of control, and because the trainers can be expected to be experts in the artificial system and hence able to teach it. Most organization-run training is "orders in another form."

When training is conducted by people from outside the organization, as it increasingly is, or by trainers within the organization who have studied with those from without, the subject matter is frequently wholly or in part the natural system (usually natural systems of organizations in general). For the most part, external students of organizations use a natural-system model and study the organization as a complex of statistical distributions. The values they import into their science, and hence into their training programs, are natural-system values—that is, natural laws. Furthermore, they are observers rather than participants and so have interests different from organization members. Understanding is more important than profit (or success defined in some other way). Furthermore, they do not have to take responsibility for the results of their advice. Usually they are academics, and since few people pay any attention to them outside the classroom, they feel free to say whatever they want.

From these outside (and perhaps inside) trainers, therefore, trainees absorb some forbidden fruit. They learn about the natural system, and they may learn natural-law values—such as that of the natural harmony of the organization, or that one should be "people-oriented" rather than "task-oriented," or that their organization is "unhealthy." Natural systems are only dimly understood by participants, though much of their behavior is controlled by them. Armed with this new knowledge, the trainee may attempt to resist organization controls or to manipulate them for personal or group

advantage. Or he may wish to realize his new natural law values—
e.g., being people-oriented rather than production-oriented. In
either case, he cannot be fully trusted by either his peers or his
superiors. He may have become more of an observer than a participant and hence not quite trustworthy from the organization stand-
point. Tremendous pressure will be put upon him to return to the
old, safe, predictable, pretraining role performance. In a few
months his training will probably have "washed out." If not, his
frustrations may induce him to resign or seek a transfer, or he may
be fired.[15] The potential conflict between the external criteria—the
owner's goals—and the survival criteria of the natural system is
real and inescapable. Tools are not designed to survive or to
be happy. Etzioni adds the point that human-relations (natural-
system) training for foremen assumes that they can be both formal
leaders (who are officers of the company) and informal leaders of
the men—that they can play influence roles in both the artificial and
natural systems. The resulting conflict and stress will render such
dual roles intolerable for all but a very small number of very un-
usual people.[16]

5 SOLUTIONS

Smaller Units

A more irrational reaction to the impersonality of modern organizations is the growth of a spirit of regression to a simpler technology and hence simpler organization forms. Even as the British textile workers of the early nineteenth century followed "General Ludd" in his destruction of new labor-saving technology, many today wish to blame science and technology not only for such problems as pollution but also for the alienation, the frustration and desperation, of the individual. (I should say "some individuals" since most, I suspect, are doing very well.) Commitment to this position seems to be associated with fanaticism, with the charisma of a "movement," and as such it shows a tendency to follow the ancient fallacy that the end justifies the means. There have been suggestions of conscious distortions, even by scientists, by those opposing the Amchitka underground blast, the use of DDT, the SST—and who knows what else? We are told that there are currently (1972) ten times as many college students enrolled in classes teaching astrology as in classes teaching astrophysics.[1] The 1970 and 1971 annual meetings of the American Association for the Advancement of Science were disrupted several times by groups who had defined the enemy as a personified "science" and blamed it for everything from human failure to racial prejudice to war. But if scientists are moving in the wrong direction, it is because they are allowing bureaucrats, politicians, college administrators, and private Luddite groups to define that direction, to push their research in directions contrary to their scientific instincts.

Under pressure from "environmentalists" all during 1971, the Atomic Energy Commission was forced into a major reorganization, the purposes of which, according to AEC Chairman James R. Schlesinger, were to deemphasize "technology purely for the sake of technology" and to "provide increased emphasis on environmental matters and on research . . . on . . . various aspects of safety."[2] The danger of politically directed research is the loss of redundancy and hence reliability. Substituted for the decisions of many scientists and technologists following their own interests is the decision or conclusion of a bureaucrat or a politician, or a group or institution composed of them. Such decisions have a very high chance of being proved wrong over the long run. The age of the prophets was in the Biblical past.

It is difficult to imagine a more dangerously mistaken view than this neo-Ludditism. Science and technology are simply knowledge about how to solve problems. Self-imposed ignorance can do nothing for anyone. Translated into economic terms, the plea for scientific, technical, and hence industrial regression is a plea for increased unemployment and inflation. Human problems are bound to increase, requiring ever more knowledge and ingenuity. Disillusionment with the older romanticism of progress does not necessarily imply an hysterical despair. In fact, it requires quite the opposite.

Technological development has produced an ever larger and more expensive material component (the "hardware") and this fact has necessarily resulted in ever larger organizations, ever more centralization. (Of course, the desire for power has had the same effect and in some cases has increased size and centralization far beyond what can be justified technically.) Only a science-fiction-type technological breakthrough—like a breast-pocket computer, perhaps—could reverse this trend toward increasing organization size and centralization. Such an eventuality cannot be predicted one way or the other, but on the basis of our past history we cannot expect it,[3] at least in manufacturing. (The growth of service industry may reverse this trend, as discussed below.)

Appreciation of the impersonal (dehumanizing?) consequences of size has led to suggestions to decentralize and to operate from smaller units. There is much evidence to the effect that small units are more comfortable working milieux. An organization in which each person can get to know most of the others personally has many of the qualities of a club, if not indeed of a family. Authority relations are softened by various social relations that develop concomitantly. Evaluations and penalties are leavened by the emotions and obligations of something approaching friendship. The same is true for interpersonal competition and hence communication. Secrecy is much less important where win/lose competition is actually taboo, a breech of community relations, of good neighborship. Knowledge of the total operation is more easily had by everyone, providing each worker with a cognitive map that helps to restore the meaningfulness of work. In these small organizations the natural system may become so strong as to dominate the artificial system. The owner and his plans may come to be at the mercy of the natural system (or, as some would say, the informal organization).

The small unit is likely to be less impersonal and more compassionate toward the client or customer. Roles are more general and hence relations less restricted. Having fewer customers promotes familiarity. Final decisions can be reached lower in a hierarchy and hence perhaps more quickly. Procedures are likely to be simpler and more easily modified on the spot if they threaten to bring about absurdities. All these things will help the client or customer feel more like a person and less like a problem category. He is likely to think such an organization is a "good" one, i.e., a compassionate one.

There have been a number of predictions that the organization of the future is going to be smaller, impermanent, and democratic,[4] but it is possible that these predictions are mere wishful thinking. The evidence is not clear. I agree that whenever the technology of the task allows decentralization into small units, the correct ethical position is to propose or support such decentralization. Task technology in advertising, movie and television-program making, and similar activities has long promoted a type of organization that I shall call project organization.

Project organization not only allows the greater personalism (compassion) of the small organization, but it has other apparent values. Professor Samuel P. Huntington of Harvard reports that by 1958 the technical (read "strategic") problems of war had been settled in this country, stabilizing the large defense bureaucracies within which the survival ("bureaucratic") needs of individuals and groups had to be met. In that year, the technical ("strategic") functions fell within no single service but within interservice functional commands.[5] The "bureaucratic" rivalry stemming from survival needs (career needs, if you prefer) was no longer reinforced by technical considerations. To put it another way, bureaucratic, interservice, career-type rivalries no longer needed to interfere with technical (strategic) problem solving. Strategic flexibility was acquired by separating bureaucratic survival needs from the structure for technical problem solving, that is, by placing technical problem solving in temporary project organizations (although they are not so called by the military).

Project organization separates the homeostatic, equilibrating, adaptive foot dragging of the natural system (dominated by the internal criterion of survival) and the instrumental, expansive, prescriptive problem solving of the artificial system (dominated by the externally generated and imposed goals of the owner—in the case of the military or any other public organization, by the public and the public interest). Because components of the project organization (group, team, etc.) can fall back on their permanent bureaucratic home for survival "career" needs, they will be less resistant to changes of an instrumental or technical nature, and in the case of the military, less resistant to strategic innovations.

In recent years there have been an increasing number of small research, development, and engineering organizations that, meeting the criterion for small size, have been humane and even exciting places for professional and subprofessional personnel to work.[6] Many of these have even met the test of impermanence, either because they worked on one or a few contracts at a time and were constantly forming and reforming in response to immediate, specific, contractual, and subcontractual needs, or because their experienced staff, in high demand, could often play a game of musical chairs (encouraged by government contract rules that allowed much higher salaries and raises for new personnel than for old: the more times you changed jobs, the richer you became). The world of these small, changing organizations is a world of personal friendships and loyalties, of greatly rewarding mutual admiration, and consequently of powerful mutual and self-controls. Such organizations are not bureaucracies in Max Weber's sense of the term.

No one knows how many opportunities for project organization exist within our huge bureaucracies or whether such opportunities are increasing. Although this question is one of unimaginable importance, it has never been researched, to my knowledge. One area in which the general project pattern is most applicable and is perhaps beginning to appear is in that of new-product development in business. The bureaucratic structure is deadly here.[7] The survival need most threatened, in addition to the hostilities and plottings of one's apprehensive peers, is security. Yesterday's entrepreneur risked (somebody else's) money; if he failed he could move elsewhere and try again. With vastly improved data gathering, storage, and transmittal by an enormous credit-rating industry, today's failed entrepreneur is less likely to get a second chance. Entrepreneurship, therefore, must largely take place inside huge bureaucracies, which are also more likely to have the vastly increased amounts of capital needed. Today's entrepreneur, consequently, is usually an official—a bureaucrat. If he fails, he loses more than money: his failure goes into his personnel record and follows him around forever. This record, as Erving Goffman has said, is a part of him; it is his paper alter ego. When he fails, therefore, the bureaucratic entrepreneur loses part of his personality, his ego, his image— losses infinitely more important than money, which Shakespeare rightly said was trash by comparison.

The bureaucrat entrepreneur usually does not know what the outcome of a new product venture will be. Most ventures fail,[8] and even the successes take so long to register success that the original recommender, the bureaucratic entrepreneur, may have been charged with failure or retired long before. Even if he had some rough notions of the probability of success, he has no knowledge of the outcome of this particular case, this particular toss of the coin. What would be rational for the organization, which lives in the long run, would not be rational for him, given our doctrines of administrative responsibility.[9] His rationality dictates a search for immediate profitability. The two rationalities—that of the organization and that of our would-be entrepreneur—are mathematically distinct. Under our concept of individualized, exclusive administrative responsibility, the risk of the official is so great that for him to recommend a new-product venture would be nonrational.

The problem of developing new products, therefore, is one of (1) recognizing and motivating entrepreneurial talent (a propensity for high risk?), (2) reducing individual risk, and (3) finding and releasing creative capacity. Business organizations fit along a continuum in their blindly groping attempts to solve this problem organizationally. At one extreme is the organization with a stable product, technology, and market that barely recognizes that such a problem exists. Automobile manufacturers would be examples. An early approach to the problem was a purely bureaucratic one: establish a division to deal with it—the New-Products Division.[10] This response to a problem is undoubtedly the most characteristic bureaucratic response: perception of problem ——→ assign responsibility for its solution to some individual ——→ place a bureaucratic organization at his disposal. Thus, if a superintendent of schools is running into increasing criticism about racial prejudice, it is a good possibility that he will appoint an "assistant superintendent for racial problems" (or civil rights, or what not).[11] In fact, as I will show later, this response is becoming increasingly alluring as a solution to the problem of administrative compassion: an official, often called an ombudsman, is appointed to deal with it.

The next step in the development of organizational adaptations to the new-products problem, and probably representing a greater degree of urgency for its solution, is to adopt the older project form as copied from advertising, and appoint "new-product managers." The most recent organization adaptation, coming from the organizations with the greatest need to solve the new-products problem— large, high-technology organizations, like the big chemical companies—is the "venture group."[12] In this adaptation, a group of highly trained business and scientific (including engineering) professionals are brought together, given a largely nonaccountable budget ("funny money"), assured of their power to commandeer the services of the permanent bureaucratic functional divisions, and physically removed from the premises for as long (reasonably) as it takes to come up with a new product and bring it to the level of marketability. Some groups have even been legally separated, financed, and launched as independent companies. Venture groups have been known to remove themselves to peaceful surroundings conducive to creativity, such as beautiful seashores. This system works best of all, provided authorities back in the bureaucratic homeland can keep the sword of Damocles from hanging over the venture group's head. Creation can be neither coerced nor crassly purchased.[13]

Many people feel that customers were well treated during economic depressions. Businesses were so eager for sales that they would go out of their way to help customers. But when ours became a full-employment economy, so the theory goes, many store clerks acted as if they could not care less whether they made a sale. These perceptions, and others like them, give rise to the belief in competition. Competition will cure the impersonality, the lack of compassion, of large organizations. Customers and clientele can shop around until they find the kind of treatment they crave.[14]

Government activities, however, are monopolies. The science of administration seeks to eliminate overlapping and duplication; it seeks to divide up the work and parcel it out in exclusive jurisdictions so that if anything goes wrong the person to blame can be identified. As Martin Landau has said, the management ideal is zero redundancy.[15] Until this state is reached, there is some "waste" in the system. The reliability that natural systems derive from redundancy is to be derived in artificial systems from elaborately contrived control devices. Artificial systems depend upon management.

Consequently, competition within the bureaucracy appears to Congress, the President, staff agencies, and the press as duplication and overlapping—as waste. Furthermore, though some governmental activities are services that might (I think they would) be improved by competition (e.g., education, street cleaning, garbage collection), it is difficult to imagine competition in most government activities: armies, police, economic regulation, subsidies, elections, planning and zoning, building and other code enforcement, foreign policy, etc. Usually, though not always, government services arise because of a breakdown of competition.[16]

Consequently, that great stimulus to good service, competition, is lacking in government and to restore it would in most cases entail removing the activity from the public sector and putting it in the private one. All interaction involves some cost. If the parties to the interaction are equal in power, the costs must be shared. If most of the power is on one side—if the interaction is monopolistic, as interactions with government nearly always are—the bureaucracy can and does shift the cost to the clientele.[17] When the client is kept waiting for hours and is then, as likely as not, told to come back tomorrow; when having worked up from the end of one line, a client is sent back to the end of another on the ground that he is in the wrong line; when a form is rejected for a minor error and the client is told to go back home and fill it out right; when a suspect is pushed around in a back room of a police station—when such things happen, the monopolistic bureaucracy is shifting the cost of the interaction to the client. When a fiercely competitive retailer establishes and enforces the policy that "the customer is always right," the costs of the interaction have been largely shifted to the store clerks and away from the customers. As Golda Meir said not too long ago: "Bureaucracy is not unique to Israel and we did not invent it. But we do have unenviable achievements in the field. How can an official tell someone coming to his office to return again tomorrow, or next week, to telephone or to write a letter, when all that official has to do is to step to the next room and clear up the matter on the spot? Why must it be the immigrant [or any other client] who has to do all the running around?"[18]

An example of cost shifting is the widespread use of lie-detector tests in industry: "The average lie-detector test costs $25, compared with more than $100 for a background check, according to Saul D. Astor, president of Management Safeguards, Inc., a consulting firm that specializes in loss prevention. 'As a result,' he said, 'polygraph examinations have become a routine part of doing business for many corporations of all types and sizes across the country.' "[19]

The last two suggestions for increasing administrative compassion, for personalizing the treatment of individuals by organizations—decentralizing and establishing competition in the supply of service—suggest that a more comfortable and individualized administration could be purchased for a price. If we were willing to accept less for our dollar, we could go to the corner grocery instead of the supermarket. In government circles and in political science it is often said that if the individual does not like the impersonal, cate-gorized, statistical treatment that he receives from administrative agencies, he can go to the courts and there get individualized, per-sonal, unique treatment. This argument, seemingly plausible be-cause of the large amount of time and money spent by courts on individual cases, is false. In the first place, going to court is too time-consuming and expensive to be feasible for most people. Mak-ing an administrative appeal or writing a letter to one's congress-man, inadequate as such actions are, gives the ordinary individual a better chance of success.

More important, however, is the fact that courts of law are in-stitutionalized to seek the general principle in the individual case. Justice is blind. The individual is unimportant; only the principle counts. (Juries, of course, modify this statement somewhat.) One of the hardest lessons the young law student must learn is to give up his natural, compassionate interest in the outcomes and disposi-tions for the actual persons involved in the cases he studies and to learn to concentrate solely on the principles of law involved.

After three years of practice in reading cases from this perspec-tive, the law student acquires the professional capacity to exclude from consideration the personal and compassionate aspects of the case, much as the young medical student learns to stand the sight of blood and the thought of pain and death. This skill in imperson-ality is a necessary prerequisite to the successful practice of the pro-fession—the giving of good legal advice and the healing of minds and bodies. Full feedback of information from clients would make the practice of both law and medicine impractical—and also, of course, the practice of warfare.[20]

Since courts are staffed almost completely by law students grown older and professionally successful, one can safely argue that the court system is the least compassionate of all of our institutions. (I will have more to say about government by courts at a later point.)

In an earlier time, the specific social position of the individual was so important that all administrative action had to be tailored to individual cases. Except for the lower classes, clients were not mere problem categories. Only when this form of social differentia-tion had declined enormously was it possible to begin planning efficient administration using universal rules, forms, and procedures for whole problem classes of people.[21] The modern administrative norm, which made efficient administration possible, was the rule that everyone in the same problem category should be treated equally. The result of the norm was to strip away the uniquenesses of individuals and to turn administration into an efficient business of mass processing of cases within each problem category. This resulted in an enormous lowering of unit costs plus other valuable consequences, such as predictability. Thus, the norm was a necessary prerequisite of modern, mass-democratic government.

This equalizing quality of modern administration is especially apparent in people-processing organizations, such as mental hospitals and prisons, in which budgetary limitations require that the official staff of functionaries be small relative to the number of people to be processed. It becomes necessary for the staff to "strip" the people to be processed ("inmates") of nearly all individuating characteristics and to treat all of them practically the same, except for differences dictated by the goals, routines, and problem categories of the organization. Only a minimum of variety in clothes, food, furnishings, or recreation can be effectively administered on such tightly controlled budgets. It all becomes G.I.[22]

Nearly all administrative organizations have these same problems, though not in such an extreme form, and must resort to some of the "stripping" tactics of the more total institutions. They apply the norm of equality. Even in nondemocratic governments of industrial nations the norm is applied to everyone but the political elite. The "rule of law" in this sense is an administrative necessity in an industrial country. Industrialism is impossible without the lowered unit costs and increased predictability that result. Though it is too late for industrialized and industrializing nations, there are countries that still can choose between personalized, individualized, compassionate administrative treatment of at least some of the population (generally, the aristocracy or others able to buy compassion) and administrative efficiency. For us, it is simply too late.

6 SOLUTIONS

Combining Roles

One set of proposed solutions to the administrative-compassion problem (among other problems) involves combining the roles of owner and functionary, or owner and customer-client, in the same person. Where this solution involves no more than the suggestion for small, independent businesses, it has already been discussed as part of the suggestion that we have smaller organizations. Where this suggestion is made in regard to larger organizations, it requires some special attention.

The suggestion for combining roles is closely related to a confusion between associations and organizations. Much "organization theory" and research is about associations, not organizations. The distinction is very important. Associations require a number of people with a shared interest—not an interest in common. For example, a number of people may share an interest in bird watching, in worshiping God, in farming. Each can pursue this interest alone or in association with others. On the other hand, a group with a common interest would have a common goal. It would be, at least incipiently, an organization.

In addition to there being a shared interest, a precondition for an association is communication between the people who have the shared interest so that they become aware of the fact that they have it. Out of this communication must grow a commitment to organize to promote the shared interest. Constitutional procedures must be developed and accepted to govern these communications, the criteria of membership, the organizing, and the distributing and controlling of power among the members. The constitution gives legitimacy to the undertaking; it provides for the validation of association policy and procedure and for settling internal disputes.

Even after all of these steps have been completed, our association is still not an organization because it still lacks a goal. The goal is formed through the use of constitutional procedures. These legitimize and call forth the obligations of members based on the commitment to the association that is already given and implied by virtue of their membership. The processes of goal formation and change are what we call politics. They concern power acquisition, maintenance, and use.

Once the goal (or goals) is set, a system for achieving it must be be designed. Designing requires, in principle, an organization designer—a technician who knows how to design such a tool. The association is the owner—at this point, the client of the designer. The design, which is an artificial (manmade) prescriptive system, may be simple or elaborate, depending upon the goal, the technology currently believed to be available for achieving it, the obstacles to achieving it (constraints), and the degree of goal accomplishment desired by the owner. Functionary roles are created as part of the design. Increasingly, these roles are simply selected from the culture and are a result of the upgrading, standardizing, and professionalizing of work. With all of these steps, the association has created within itself an organization to implement its goals.

The association now has the capacity to make choices—to make decisions and carry them out. A division occurs between the association and its decisional organs, between the owner and its tool. The latter develops separate interests that are related to the personal and group needs of the incumbents of the constituted roles and are often in conflict with those of the owner (the association). Association members may play functionary roles or they may hire others to do so. Both methods are often used, as when politically elected functionaries appoint the rest.

Everything we have said so far about modern bureaucracy applies to the bureaucracy (the tool) of our association. There is an externally imposed goal. Modern administrative norms and designs will dominate. Natural systems to protect personal and group interests of the functionaries will develop. Conflict will develop between the owner's goal and norms of efficiency, on the one side, and the survival or conservation needs of functionaries, on the other—conflict between the natural and artificial systems. In the modern period, implementation of goals will be impersonal, professional, efficient, and universalistic rather than compassionate. But what if all functionary roles, or all customer/client roles, are really filled by association members—by the owners? Will we then get compassionate administration?

Before attempting to answer this question I should point out that there is sometimes a false perception of the combination of owner and functionary (or customer) roles. Occasionally some participants in organizations (or participants in some organizations) lose sight of their social moorings and come to believe they are untouchable—part of an autonomous community independent of outside evaluation, power, and control—independent of outside "ownership."

The sociologist Philip Selznick refers to this development as institutionalization; he accepts the organic, consumatory, noninstrumental nature of some organizations—those that have become so institutionalized that they have acquired an expressive significance for both the members and the community. Rather than being mere tools, he feels, some organizations become natural systems and therefore come to need organs for developing and choosing their own goals. The organ he chooses is the top "leader." Presumably all organizations should so develop into institutions (natural systems), but only a very few actually do so. Institutions are not dispensable like tools, he says, and criteria such as efficiency or cost/benefit analysis are subordinated to the criterion of survival.[1] In this treatment of organizations, Selznick is following an enduring sociological bias in favor of natural-system models that goes back to Auguste Comte, the "father of sociology." At least some organizations, Selznick seems to say, are "small societies."

This perceptual transformation of the role of organizations and their participants from instruments into autonomous organic beings is very observable in colleges and universities. Many functionaries of these collectivities think of themselves as members of self-governing communities and practically defy external forces to interfere with them. This feeling or perception of independence—of combining owner and functionary roles, like a band of thieves or a sovereign state—is reinforced in the case of the university by tradition, physical and cognitive separation from the rest of the community, long-standing norms of independence (such as the norm of academic freedom), and a feeling of moral and intellectual superiority. The last of these reinforcements dates from an early artistocratic era when trade was considered tawdry and those engaged in it a lesser breed of selfish and uncultured oafs—members of lower orders.

In recent years, some members of the academic community have wrapped their moral self-righteousness and intellectual superiority around themselves like cloaks of armor and defied legislatures, courts, and the taxpayers at large. They seemed to have felt invincible in their virtue. They were encouraged in this fantasy by students who saw this academic self-conception as a possible lever for prying loose more power for themselves.

The response of the community at large has been a gradual reassertion of its "ownership," of its right to define the goals of the university. The freedom and independence of the university are things of the past. It is rapidly becoming an organization, a bureaucracy, not a community, an instrument rather than what Selznick calls an institution. It is becoming expendable.

But let us get back to bona fide cases of combining owner and functionary or owner and customer/client roles. If these roles were truly combined, would the result be a more compassionate administration? The resulting organization would be no different in principle from any other modern bureaucracy. Norms would sharply differentiate the private from the public—the functionary's rights and duties from those of the owner. Conflicts between the "owner's" goals ("his" interests) and those of the functionaries would still occur, as when the owner-operator of a service station struggles with himself over whether to close early and go to play golf. Rules to help solve such role conflicts have evolved, as when doctors are taught never to treat members of their own family. The owners' interest in efficient goal accomplishment will encourage them to adopt and apply to themselves as functionaries all the devices of modern, efficient administration: strict accounting, personnel-administration practices such as pay-according-to-performance ratings, etc.

Owners who are acting also as customers, say in co-ops, will not be expected to be treated "particularistically" and given special prices—in fact, there will be especially strong taboos, even laws, against such attempts. The functionaries, whether owners or not, will show the human tendencies to generate an interpersonal system (the natural system) whose only criterion is survival, not the owner's (their) goals. The functionaries of a union, themselves union members, will form a union-within-a-union and engage in unionlike activities, including strikes.

People who study the subject claim that cutting functionaries into a piece of the ownership, as in profit sharing, will mitigate the natural conflict between owners and functionaries, between the artificial system and the natural system. I believe that the evidence sustains this claim, but it is important to note that the conflict is only mitigated.[2]

When the same person performs two naturally conflicting roles, conflicts are not eliminated. They are often resolved by psychological rather than political methods, which makes the conflict resolution less visible and hence more difficult to understand.[3] Such conflicts, however, are frequently resolved by political methods, half the members choosing to emphasize its functionary role and half its ownership role. In fact, I think it not too much to say that all political conflict can be interpreted as role conflict, meaning that a choice between roles must be made by each individual before a particular political conflict becomes possible. Israelis may fight Arabs, but each participant in the struggle must decide first whether to play the role of an Israeli (or Arab), on the one hand, or that of a human being, on the other (not to mention the numerous other role choices of citizen-family member, age-group-national, sex-national, and so on and on). In the India-Pakistan war of late 1971, several role choices had to be made—national, religious, and ideological—before the conflict could be joined. About half of the refugees who fled to India did not want to go back to an independent Bangladesh. And note the complex role choices in the Irish conflict. By selecting religion as the role criterion, Senators James Buckley and Edward Kennedy, at odds on most issues, could agree on the desirability of British withdrawal and the incorporation of northern Ireland (Ulster) into Eire (Ireland).

Organizations that combine crucial roles in the same persons (e.g., co-ops, unions), usually become big, impersonal, abstract, and noncompassionate, just as other bureaucracies do, and for the same reasons, and with the same results. (Some of the Watergate villains were milk-marketing co-ops!) In the final analysis, a co-op, for example, is just another method of financing some activity. It has no implication whatever for our problem of administrative compassion. As for a union bureaucracy, complaints by functionaries are likely to be met with Harry Truman's famous maxim: if you can't stand the heat, stay out of the kitchen. As to the people and entities with whom the union deals, a compassionate union is either corrupt or—like the lion in the Wizard of Oz— hilarious.

7 SOLUTIONS

Political Machines and Prefectural Administration

Any purposive social entity has two classes of problems to solve. One class relates to achieving its goal, and is often called the "instrumental" class of problems. The other class involves keeping the social entity together so that it can solve its instrumental problems. Keeping it together is often called the "maintenance" class of problems. Solving maintenance problems is logically prior to solving instrumental ones.[1]

Under some political conditions, delicate treatment of clientele groups seems to be a political necessity. Maintaining the consensual basis of a political community looms as a larger problem, in the eyes of the political elite, than efficient administrative problem solving. Administrative resources are used for reasons of political maintenance. Administration is compassionate, inefficient, and "corrupt."[2] (The quotes around "corrupt" are needed, I think, because whether an action is defined as corrupt depends on the existence of widely held norms defining it as "corrupt." If the sign says "no tipping," then tipping is "bribery" and is "corrupt.")

Conditions such as these existed in the United States after the Civil War when massive immigration into newly forming cities, both from within and from abroad, created low-consensus, heterogeneous political communities with great problem-solving needs. A workable level of consensus was created through "corrupt political machines," which traded administrative resources for political support (consensus). Thus were the cities built, and in just a few decades.[3]

Conditions similar to those just described still exist in countries such as France and Italy.[4] The basic political issues have never been resolved. Political consensus is below the level needed to handle many modern problems. Approximately a quarter of the electorate in those two countries normally vote communist—vote, that is, to destroy the constitution by bloody violence.[5] (Of course, many, if not most, of these voters probably do not think of their vote for a communist as meaning precisely this.) The use of administrative resources, including compassion, to purchase a necessary minimal consensus appears to be a necessity even as it did during the boss-machine period of city politics in America. The administrative solution in many of these politically divided countries is the prefectoral system of field administration.[6]

Prefectoral field administration has its origins in the functional requirements of an earlier period and continues to exist, if not purely as ritual, because no substitutes for many of those functions have been found. In earlier periods of low technology, government performed only a few functions (keeping civic order, providing for military defense, collecting taxes, and perhaps maintaining roads and communications in aid of the others).[7] Because of a lack of communication and transportation, citizens were organized into territorially based social organizations—into families, lineages, clans, tribes, neighborhoods, or other communal-type social structures. National consciousness was often lacking and the government official was epitomized in the tax collector or the policeman—in someone to "get around," to mollify by gifts and by insisting upon whatever prerogatives were associated with whatever relationship existed between the client and the official, such as the very common kinship relationship. One's kin in government were expected to use their administrative resources on behalf of one's needs.[8]

Under these circumstances, administration (usually a synonym for government) was territorially organized, whether government was indigenous or imposed by a colonial power. Let us use as an example the "steel frame" of British colonial administration (so called because it was used practically without exception in all British colonies and possessions).[9] A governor represented the British monarch in the country. He had full government powers; he was a "viceroy," a little king, and he ran a sort of court with the usual pomp and ceremony.

The country was subdivided into provinces, in turn divided into districts. At the head of each province was a commissioner, the representative of the governor, a little viceroy or king in his province. The district was governed by the agent of the commissioner (sometimes commissioners did not amount to much and the district head was the true representative of the governor). This district agent was usually called the district officer (D.O.) or the district commissioner (D.C.). As the viceroy in the district, he dealt with the "natives" and had full power of government—the full power of the king-governor-commissioner in his small area. He personified the distant majesty and ran his own court where he (his gracious Lady hovering in the background) dispensed justice, collected taxes, settled disputes, jailed and punished, supervised and taught the natives some simple arts of government.

The district officer watched out for political dissension and had the native force to handle it, usually, but he could always call upon the forces of the viceroys in the higher territories, up to the army of the king. If administrative services were needed—say, a new track through the woods, a new community meeting hall, or what not—the D.O. was money raiser, planner, engineer, and supervisor of the project, all in one. The outcome could be no better than the skills of this untrained man permitted (he was frequently out of a classical education at "Oxbridge"), but even this was often technically superior to what the "natives" could have done on their own.

As knowledge, technology, specialization, and needs rapidly accumulated, especially in the twentieth century, there grew up around the governor a host of specialized ministries dealing in specialized subjects and staffed by technically trained specialists in education, health, finance, economic development, community development, agriculture, etc., as needs appeared and skills became available.[10] Agents of these ministries were eventually located in the districts, the better to bring their skills to bear on local problems.

As district officers lost their real functions to specialists from the ministries, one after the other, the legal fiction was maintained that the D.O. was still the "viceroy," still legally omnicompetent, and that all the specialists were really under his direction as part of "the district team." Meetings of the "team" were called less and less frequently, as the ability of the district officer, both to define a district policy goal and to supervise its implementation, gradually withered away. After all, it would have been foolish for a D.O. to insist on drawing the plans for a new meeting house, infirmary, or school when a real architect from the central ministry was available.

District officers still had a function, however. They lost one administrative problem-solving function after another to experts, but they could still perform important political-maintenance functions for the central government.[11] They could warn of growing dissension, and perhaps put it down. Law and order, control of elections, and supervision of local governing bodies were the last functions to go. If the specialists from headquarters could not change the behavior of the "natives"—could not, that is, enforce national policy in the district—they could call upon the charisma of the D.O., the awe in which the agent of the distant Raj was still held. If the moralistic, universalistic, equal, and technically accurate application of the law violated some local custom or ancient understanding, the D.O. had the legal authority to make an exception or to modify the specialists' local programs. If he felt the political situation demanded it, he could call upon any kind of administrative resources available, including jobs for relatives of local notables.

Naturally, he was despised by the central-ministry specialists, who were trained (often in European universities) in modern administrative morals—in the norms of universalism, achievement, impersonality, equality before the law, strict fiscal accountability. The D.O., however, was performing an important political function for the distant governor, the great viceroy, and so was protected against constant complaints and plots by the central ministries to clip his wings, if not indeed to serve him up at a feast.

As the British relinquished control of their colonies after World War II, these field officers, the viceroys, were quickly nativized and in some places efforts were made to put them under civil service. However, if they had a function at all (other than a rapidly disappearing residual one), it was political, and so civil service as applied to them could only be formalistic. In most places they became frankly political officers attached to the political elite in power and sharing its political fortunes.[12] Thus, when the military took over the government of Rwanda in 1973, it kept the central civilian bureaucracy intact, but turned field administration over to army officers.

The relative power and importance of the two types of field officers, the generalist, political district officers and the technical, specialized, administrative civil service field representatives of the central ministries, therefore, depend upon the extent to which there is a national political consensus. Efficient administration, in short, is a luxury of a politically stable community organized outside its administration in such a way that it can control the administration and hold it accountable for meeting externally imposed goals efficiently.[13]

This "steel frame" of colonial, areal administrative organization may persist through historical habit. Assuming that the major problems of political maintenance, those of achieving a basic consensus sufficient to govern, are eventually resolved, an areal type of administrative organization, if it persists, is bound to become largely ritualistic. As knowledge and technology accumulate, problem-solving passes from status to expertise. Increasingly, with political problems basically solved, the power of expertise, the ability to solve problems, is what counts.[14]

Eventually, the viceroy becomes mere pageantry, and people with needs turn to those who can help them, the expert field representatives of the central ministries. Area gives way to function. Function (problem solving) does not and cannot recognize fixed areas, and if area is somehow involved in the technical solution of a problem, the size and shape of the area will be different for every type of problem (actually, every type of technology). Today, neighborhoods are being urged as the appropriate area for various welfare services, while regional governments are being considered for such things as land- and water-use control. Areas of over fifty different sizes and shapes are used in the field administration of the central government of France.

The persistence, in the long run, of fixed area-based administration, such as that of cities and states, can only be political. If citizen consensus must undergird government problem solving, citizen evaluation of a general government's overall performance is probably all that can be expected. Evaluation and consent, function by function, is now—and I think will remain—far too complex for citizens. Until consent (consensus) is no longer relevant to government, therefore, political needs will ensure the perpetuation of area-based government units such as cities and states. Functions will probably escape these areal traps only as political controversy concerning the functions subsides.

Prefectoral-type administrative structures persist, therefore, where basic problems of political consensus persist—in France and Italy, for example, and in the newly forming "nations" of Africa.[15] In both France and Italy, as has been noted already, a fourth of the vote normally goes to the Communist party. In both of these countries Communists sometimes win control of some city governments, whereupon the central government relies upon the local prefect to render them harmless.

In prefectural administration, the country is divided into provinces each ruled by a fully powered agent of the central government appointed by and responsible to a central minister, often the minister of the interior. In legal theory, all powers exercised over citizens in the province (in France it is called a *departement*) are those of the prefect. Specialist agents of central ministries are bitter competitors in the provinces. The prefect in turn, to protect himself, surrounds himself with divisions of counterpart experts to deal with the expert agents of the central ministries on a somewhat more equal basis.

Although the fiction of prefectoral administrative problem solving is maintained, the real function of the prefect is political. He administers elections. He and his lady maintain court where local notables can be seen. He makes exceptions to the laws and otherwise uses administrative resources to maintain a consensus (such as it is) favorable to the central government. Central-ministry experts regard him as a political meddler and are bitterly critical of him, but still rush to use his charismatic support when they have difficult problems of enforcement (i.e., problems of consensus).

Although prefects are no longer expected to manipulate elections, they are still able to exercise great influence by the partisan use of their superior political knowledge of the locality. They are also in a position to grant many minor favors, such as issuing or expediting trading or liquor licenses, and some more important favors, such as reporting favorably on large schemes for borrowing money or for local development.

Given the lack of political consensus in countries such as France and Italy, their national politicians must have local political bases and so are also, frequently, important local politicians—elected members of provincial, subprovincial or commune (municipal) councils. They need the prefect and his favors, as he needs their good reports to the minister of interior. The result is a fruitful political exchange that helps maintain the stability of government.

Provinces are subdivided into smaller areas (called *arrondissement* in France, districts in Africa), headed by a prefect's principle subordinate, the subprefect. He, too, is a viceroy in his district, a fully powered agent of the central government, subject, of course, to vetoes by the prefect and the minister of interior. His greatest power and most important role is supervision of the elected governments (mayor and council) of the communes (of which there are about 38,000 in France). This supervisory power, called *tutelage* in France, involves the vetoing of illegal acts, controlling the budget, and exercising the right to require that legally mandated actions be performed.

Many communes are so small that they lack expertise on all aspects of government and depend upon the subprefect. Many commune governments are so hopelessly divided politically that they act with complete political irresponsibility and depend upon the subprefect to protect them with his veto. In some cases, local governments are so irresponsible that the subprefect recommends that they be dissolved by the prefect. Often he works subtly with the local politicos and others to get sensible solutions to local problems.

Lack of political consensus affects all levels of government, of course, and often the prefectures must develop policies that should be developed by the central government but cannot be for political reasons. In France such prefectural policies have been developed in the fields of housing and management-labor relations; or prefects may refuse to carry out court eviction orders. In countries such as France and Italy, the prefects are politically necessary as embodiments of missing political virtues and, at the same time, as convenient scapegoats for almost everything that goes wrong.

The prefect performs many of the political functions of the former American political "boss." The conditions that made the boss functional no longer exist in the American political system. Furthermore, federalism provides two constitutional officials who perform political functions performed by prefects in prefectural governments, namely, the American governor and the American mayor. Consequently, field administrative systems in this country concentrate on administration and they are far less political than in some other countries.

It is interesting that the effort to create a nonpolitical municipal executive in this country (in the form of expert city managers) has been successful only in communities low in political conflict. Most city managers have been unable to escape politics and their tenure has depended upon political contingencies.[16]

Performance of political functions by mayors and governors (and by the President) stimulates criticism, almost contempt, for them on the part of "good government" people. It is much like the criticism and contempt directed toward the prefects. There is a feeling that good government should be nonpolitical. When we send advisers to the heads of developing countries, we almost invariably send problem-solving experts whose advice often cannot be followed because it neglects the problems of political maintenance, which are by far the most pressing ones facing these political heads.[17]

The most relevant "expert" we have is the person who knows how to solve *both* kinds of problems, who knows how to assemble the needed amounts of both political consensus and administrative (problem-solving) resources to get done the things that need doing. Since there are so few of this type left in the United States, one is tempted to observe that perhaps the best "expert" we could send abroad to aid the developing nations would be Mayor Richard Daley of Chicago.

It has been suggested that the areal principle in administration may stage somewhat of a comeback in this country. "At the federal level," Herbert Kaufman writes, "this will mean renewed attempts to set up much stronger regional representatives of heads of cabinet departments than any we have had in the past. It will also mean intensified efforts to establish regional presidential representatives in the field. Similarly, we may anticipate [that] Governors and their department heads will follow the same strategies with respect to regions within the states. At the local level, Mayor [John] Lindsay has already sought . . . to win approval for 'little city halls' throughout New York."[18]

Such suggestions are based on the belief that bureaucracies have acquired too much political power and independence from the political chief executive at a time of growing dissatisfaction with bureaucratic performance by groups recently struggling to get a foothold in the political system of this country, especially blacks and, the latest arrivals on the municipal scene, Latinos. Bureaucracy has been accused of being not merely unresponsive to these interests but actually incapable of understanding them.[19] New organized interests in such fields as environmental protection have not been satisfied with bureaucratic responses to their concerns. An inchoate "youth interest," with an antibureaucratic orientation, is fast developing. In short, the consensus underlying a professional, nonpolitical administration has weakened. Consequently, some resurgence of interest in area (prefectural) administration is predictable.

This interest comes a little late. It is regressive. Technical complexity has developed too far. The district officer—"Sanders of the River"—cannot come back. We cannot go back to the omnicompetent father of our childhood. Today, in any particular problem situation, the generalist is simply the more ignorant person. Regional heads of holding-company-type departments, such as Health, Education, and Welfare, are little more than administrative service officers. Unable to define a regional position, their functions become either clerical or ritualistic. Communication follows functional, problem-solving routes regardless of what organization charts and instructions say.

Areal administrators are a little late for political (or are they historical?) reasons, as well. They would not only challenge other highly developed political institutions such as parties, legislatures, and interest groups, but also, in the United States, governors and mayors. Whereas, superficially, an areal representative of the President would seem to strengthen his hand by giving him an independent channel of communication to the field, experience shows that problem-solving communication follows problem-solving, functional channels. Unless they could find political work to do for the President, these areal administrators would be mere figureheads.

Even assuming that other established political institutions allowed the President to build a personal political machine out of general field civil servants throughout the country (and they probably would not),[20] he would soon lose control of these "servants" as they developed their own autonomous bases of political power. "As regional officers get more and more involved in regional complexes," Kaufman has predicted, "they will become more and more ambassadors from the regions to the chief executives instead of the executive's men in the regions. Regional differences and competition will become sources of irritation and controversy. Moreover, regional posts may become convenient and effective springboards to elective office."[21]

Such areal administrators, if they could be established, could only become political agents of the President, politically "interfering" in the processes of administration in the interest of his political ambitions. They would be sabotaged at every turn by the field civil service. They could not maintain their permanent civil-service standing but would become analogous to field cabinet officers. The President would be less able to control them than he is able to control his cabinet (central control of areal administrators is a problem that has never, in all human history, been solved for long). Violations of modern administrative norms, especially the norm of equal (noncompassionate) treatment, would bring the media down on the administrators' heads and create more trouble than help for the President. All this is in addition to the fact that legislatures (and especially legislators, who represent areal interests) and local-*area* party organizations, simply would not tolerate them. Attempts to create regional administrative coordinating mechanisms have produced nothing more substantial than luncheon clubs.[22]

The newer groups seeking a political foothold and greater political power—especially blacks and Latinos—find the area principle temporarily advantageous and consequently advocate decentralized control of important administrative activities: education, poverty programs, urban renewal and planning, police, etc. Many members of these groups have not been socialized to the modern administrative culture. Consequently, they perceive that administrative institutions are not sufficiently responsive to their needs.

Furthermore, ascriptive norms and arrangements are to their immediate advantage. Achievement ("merit") norms do not help them as much as they would like. These groups too, therefore, are beginning to urge a regression to the area principle in the form of neighborhood schools and other services controlled by the neighborhood residents (though financed by the "establishment"). While these groups are becoming mobilized they are not being assimilated to the dominant culture. Consequently, they are separatist, particularistic, ascriptive. It is expedient for them to be so.[23]

Even if this kind of areal decentralization were successful in temporarily reducing the frustrations of these newcomers to the political game, it could not last. The country as a whole has gone beyond the institutions of the preindustrial culture. Even if services were controlled by local communities in decentralized cities, even if the "owner" of the administrative units were the local separatist "neighborhood," the results would be almost immediately unsatisfactory. Even as colonies find political consensus evaporating once independence has been achieved, and find that they are lacking in the requisite skills, so separatist neighborhoods will find themselves lacking the political consensus and the administrative skills needed to make the dream come true. Furthermore, not being independent nations, they will find themselves in competition for money, manpower, and matériel without having the compensating powers that nationhood would provide.[24]

Beyond these practical political and administrative difficulties, there is the inescapable fact that the position of the individual vis-à-vis the bureaucratic organization would not be changed by all this political reorganization, even if it were otherwise successful. Good service is professional, impersonal, and equal—that is, universalistic and noncompassionate. The relation of the individual to this bureaucracy would be the same as to any other modern bureaucracy. Compassionate treatment of the individual would be just as rare. While impersonal, noncompassionate treatment by members of one's own race or ethnic group might seem, at first glance, more acceptable, this perception would not last; the difference from the "old days" would soon be forgotten. In fact, I suspect that bureaucratic treatment by members of one's own race (or other reference group) would be less compassionate and more impersonal, even more arbitrary, than treatment by a professionalized merit bureaucracy, one that is necessarily heavily dominated by the "other group," and one that may occasionally be motivated by a touch of guilt to "lean over backwards."

In summary, high-quality service is functionally organized. The areal generalist is professionally an ignoramus and an incompetent. Areal arrangements arise to meet political problems, not administrative ones. Current suggestions for reviving the areal principle in one form or another reflect a decline in political consensus.[25] Immediately there is a drive to use administrative resources to solve the political or consenual problem. The objective is not better-quality services, better administration, but the acquisition of political power or the trading of administrative resources for consensus. However, it is simply too late to go back to the spoils system or to other preindustrial practices. Quality administration is necessary to support our large population in the style to which it has become accustomed. The consensual problem will be solved, if at all, through our political institutions, not by raids on administration. We cannot afford the "compassionate" administration of the underdeveloped countries. Too many people would starve to death.

8 SOLUTIONS

Assign to an Office– The Ombudsman

As I noted in chapter five, the most characteristic bureaucratic response to a perceived, continuing problem is to make it the responsibility of some official and give him an organization as a tool or resource with which to deal with it. The size of the organization will depend on the amount of political pressure generated by the problem. For example, a group of local problems, under pressures arising from poverty, militancy, plus the new interest in urbanism, have been met with a new official and a new organization, the "community psychiatrist" (practicing "community psychiatry") and the Community Mental Health Center. The political steam behind these problems has generated large amounts of money for anything called "community psychiatry," even though we do not really know how to spend this money effectively. Gimmicks cannot wait upon knowledge.[1]

The problem we are discussing—the frustrations of individuals treated, with cold impersonality, as problem categories rather than as people by modern organizations—is beginning to get this typical treatment in one jurisdiction after another. I refer to the office of "ombudsman." But first let me discuss some precursors of this office in this country. For a long time, legislative representatives and their staff, at least in the Congress, have spent from one-half to three-fourths of their time receiving and trying (or pretending to try) to rectify the complaints of individual citizens from their consituencies about harsh, unfair, arbitrary, stupid, or just plain inhuman treatment by bureaucrats.

Since congressmen can become very important to bureaus, which need Congress for their funds and their legal authority, these congressional overtures on behalf of suffering citizens are taken very seriously in the bureaucracy. On November 17, 1971, the day he was confirmed as the new head of the poverty program, Phillip Sanchez sent this message to his senior staff: "Response to congressional mail takes precedence over every other item of agency business." When Elliott Richardson was head of HEW, he sent out a memo demanding prompt treatment of congressional correspondence. His memo contained a form telephone call that officials were to read over the phone to any congressman whose inquiry was not answered promptly. The official was to confess that he had been "negligent in failing to acknowledge your inquiry of —— about ——." Later he should say, "I have told Secretary Richardson that we will reply to your inquiry by ——. We will provide you with a complete and comprehensive report on ——."[2] Many argue that the protection of individuals from bureaucrats is a more important function of congressmen than planning and passing legislation.

Local communities are beginning to establish "community service officers" and offices, or some similar title, as places where citizens can go for any kind of information or any kind of complaint about local government. In December, 1971, the urban affairs subcommittee of the Joint Economic Committee of Congress proposed the establishment of some 40,000 locally elected officials and offices, federally financed, each with a jurisdiction of from 5,000 to 10,000 citizens, to help these citizens in all their dealings with the national government. The subcommittee also recommended that the President establish a special representative in each of ten regions to report to him on all community problems.

Repeatedly in the last few years, journalists, political scientists, and some lawyers have been discussing an old Swedish institution, that of the ombudsman, which was first formally established in Denmark in 1954 and was thus brought to the attention of the world.[3] The ombudsman (or his office) hears complaints of citizens about improper treatment by bureaucrats. He also discovers cases on his own during tours of inspection. The ombudsman has power to secure information from the allegedly offending agency, to make recommendations for change, and to publicize the results. In

Sweden and Denmark, the ombudsman can initiate court action against offending officials. He is supposed to be the individual's champion within giant bureaucracy. Andrew Shonfield, a British writer, associates this office with "a cult of bureaucratic humanity," and says that "the special virtue of the Ombudsman lies in the deliberate effort to impart more humanity—that is, greater concern for individual circumstances—into the behavior of administration."[4] Many Western countries, and Japan, have established this office. It is appearing in many American universities in response to student demands. Two American states, Hawaii and Nebraska, have formally established the office, and it exists in many other localities under different names.

It is difficult to evaluate this device precisely. Its very existence may have some symbolic power, deterring bureaucratic arbitrariness somewhat and perhaps affording some citizens (those who have heard about it and are not afraid of government offices) with a little sense of security. However, on the basis of what we know about bureaucracy in general and, specifically, about institutions somewhat similar to the ombudsmen, one can say with considerable confidence that the effect of the institution should not be more than barely noticeable on the just-barely-noticeable-difference scale. If the ombudsman were to be staffed in a way commensurate with the problem, his office would itself become a giant bureaucracy having all of the same problems it was supposed to cure. Setting one bureaucracy to control another, our most basic bit of administrative wisdom (called "the staff system"), only changes the locale of the problem.[5]

The office of the ombudsman well illustrates the typical bureaucratic approach to a perceived problem: assign it to an individual and give him some administrative resources (budget and organization), the amount being determined by how much political pressure is perceived to be behind the problem. It is the gimmick approach, the gimmick being a bureau or office headed by a bureaucrat. The bureaucratic gimmick takes the place of deep analysis and understanding of the problem and so leads to formalism, to a false promise and deeper frustration; and it almost guarantees that the problem will not be solved. The "administrator of administrative compassion," his office routinized, becomes an impersonal bureaucrat. The few cases he can handle do not even scratch the surface of the problem, and it is quite obvious from the statistics that everybody knows this fact and that in any case clients cannot document the kinds of frustrating and unsympathetic treatment that constitute the problem.

As of 1959, the Swedish ombudsman handled an average of 700 cases *per year,* a third of which he had to dig up himself in the course of his inspection tours (he and members of his staff manage to cover the country only once every eight years). If these figures were for the activities in his office in one city on one day, they would be interesting. Of these 700 cases, 200 are quickly dropped as unworthy, leaving about 500 cases that are pursued in an average year. About 150 of these will show "administrative errors, fault, negligence or bad faith." Only about 10 cases per year go to court; the rest are settled informally. In his first year of operation, the Danish ombudsman, whose total staff consisted of eight people, including himself and the clerks, found 18 cases of maladministration.[6]

Administrative appeals have never worked well.[7] If the reversal or correction of action depends upon officials higher in the organization, they must back up their subordinates (who usually believe they are right) or else destroy the effectiveness of their organization as a governing, problem-solving mechanism—a cost far too great to be paid in the interest of one client's feelings. If the reversal of action occurs outside the organization, in another office, like an employee's appeal to a Civil Service Commission, reprisals against the appellant are both likely and very easy to carry out. A client would usually have less to lose than an employee, but the same principle holds, and the average citizen will not take the risk.

For generations, military enlistees or conscripts have had many formal avenues of complaint, including chaplains, the Inspector General's representatives, and superior officers.[8] Studies of the American soldier during World War II indicated that, by and large, the only channel of complaint that the soldier felt it safe to use was his superior officer.[9] He did not care to risk "going around" his superior. In addition to a civil ombudsman, Sweden has a military one to protect individual members of the armed forces. As we would expect, however, the latter are hesitant to use this office, and "the overwhelming majority of the cases investigated . . . on grounds of maladministration emerge in the course of his [the military ombudsman's] personal tours of inspection."[10] In short, he has to dig them up himself. However, the real solution to the compassion and alienation problem in the military and all other total institutions is the "buddy" system and network of the "inmate" culture, which deals in all the basic needs, from extra food to love and emotional support.

An institution to correct the acts of organizations needs an independent source of information and a continuing source of power. When it must get its information from the accused organization itself, it is at the organization's mercy. There are dozens of ways of hiding, slanting, or reinterpreting incriminating information. Organization officials who could not protect their organization from an ombudsman's investigation would have to be a bit dull and naïve.[11] As for a continuing source of power, there seems to be none. Good government organizations are both weak and fickle. They go from fad to fad.

We have, as I said before, a strong tendency to seek solutions to problems by passing appropriations and establishing new bureaucratic organizations. But when bureaucracy is itself the problem, there is a prima facie case against solving the problem in this way— a rebuttable presumption against the success of such a solution. The ombudsman falls within this logical dilemma.

Even so, the ombudsman proposal deserves a fully supported try. If it does anything at all toward increasing bureaucratic monopolies' compassion towards the needs of helpless individuals, it is worthwhile.

9 SOLUTIONS

The "New Public Administration"

A far more drastic attack on the principle of administrative impersonality and objectivity, and on our governmental priorities as well, is beginning to develop within academic ranks, especially among young faculty members.[1] This group denies the possibility of a value-free social science. It declares that quantifiable, observable aspects of human relations and behavior are only partial descriptions and leave out the more important aspects of meaning and feeling. It holds that even our most basic ideas, those that seem natural and undetermined, are the products of presuppositions so fundamental as to be part of consciousness itself. It urges, therefore, that full knowledge requires an expansion of consciousness through development of full communication—communication of both facts and feelings without reservation, without self-serving suppressions and distortions designed as weapons in a battle of each against all. Consequently, it rejects positivism and the philosophy of science and toys with ideas from the philosophy of existentialism and phenomenology.[2]

Since it insists that no social science is or can be value free, this "new public administration" (and "new political science" as well) urges the frank adoption of an egalitarian value system. Our teaching and research should be aimed at helping the poor and the powerless, the halt and the maimed, the "little guy" in all power relations. The basic value, therefore, is the equalization of economic and political power. In more specific terms, the basic objectives of administration should be to solve the problems of poverty and racial or ethnic prejudice.

The role of administration is to be somewhat subversive, promoting these goals regardless of congressional or presidential mandates or the wishes of the "organized interests," and being frankly political on behalf of the poor and downtrodden. Administration should be judged according to how well it serves these values rather than by its responsiveness to an unconcerned majority or its efficiency in achieving its assigned goals. The role of schools of public administration is to recruit and indoctrinate such administrators, aptly termed "short-haired radicals."

This viewpoint represents a most amazing effort to establish a new claimant in place of the owner (that is, in place of the public). It is a brazen attempt to "steal" the popular sovereignty. Regardless of congressionally or presidentially assigned goals, public administrators, according to this group, should use their resources to advance the interests of their special clienteles. They should go out into the political marketplace and seek political alliances with the poor, the students, the blacks and other racial groups, disaffected intellectuals, women's liberation groups, and I suppose prison inmates as well. If the "establishment" has enough sense to thwart this power grab, "it may be necessary for the New Public Administration to develop outside of the existing institutional framework and thinking of the university and government."[3]

Aside from the political absurdity and immaturity of this program, it would not solve the problem of compassion for the poor and downtrodden, and it would leave all the rest of us, the vast majority, with *our* problem unsolved (and presumably worse off, since the equalization could only be accomplished by taking things away from us). It would not solve the problem for the poor and downtrodden because a professionalized bureaucracy dedicated to them would still be a professionalized bureaucracy. Expert treatment is impersonal treatment; bureaucratic treatment of any kind is institutional, impersonal treatment—treatment through rules and roles.

The occasional compassionate role player would tire just as fast when dealing with the poor and downtrodden—faster, in fact, since such people are likely to possess, on the average, less of the quality of loveability than the population at large. (The Chicago Housing Authority was sued by environmentalists for "social pollution" because of the kind of people it brought into a community.) Furthermore, stepping out of the impersonal bureaucratic role can be dangerous for the role player. A perennial sequence in prison and state mental hospital administration is for guards and other officials to allow the relationship with the inmate to develop beyond the cool, official, impersonal, noncompassionate role relation and then to be unable to control the development of the new, primary, compassionate relation, with its new and essentially illegal expectations; this continues until the instabilities and incongruities of the relationship are authoritatively corrected by superiors in an ego-shattering, emotionally painful experience, followed by a period of excessive coolness and excessive noncompassion. The whole sequence is known to old hands as "getting burnt."[4]

Compassionate treatment of the poor and downtrodden is often a kind of hoax whose principal function, really, is to reduce the neurotic sense of guilt in the "more fortunate" person. What is often needed by the "less fortunate" person is a painfully enforced readjustment and reformation of a failing personality and life style (e.g., psychiatric treatment, formal schooling) that will enable him to stand on his own feet.[5] The problem is much the same as trying to "help" underdeveloped countries. There, people must be changed so that they will not only want more things but will have the skills and attitudes necessary to produce them.

Another aspect of the "new political science" and the "new public administration" is worth discussing briefly because it illustrates the illogic and indeed the danger of making a virtue out of subjectivity. ("I deny that you can divorce normative from empirical study," as one young enthusiast at a colloquium on "the new public administration" bravely shouted.) In the usual sense, our politics is characterized by negotiation, compromise, and bargaining by interested parties; this is called a "politics of contract." Contrasted to this is a "politics of love," in which confrontation rather than bargaining is used within a group of people who share a common set of absolute ethical principles.

The purpose of politics and confrontation, according to this view, is not to "win" but to assure that the political decision, the policy, is logically consistent with this absolute ethics. In Professor Theodore Lowi's verson of this process, bargaining is abolished, but the confrontation discussion is to test and gain consensus for the validity of the principle. In this way government again becomes principled (i.e., moral), and the public interest is rediscovered. Government ceases to be a by-product of private horse trading.[6]

Professor Lowi's book, *The End of Liberalism,* is a most passionate plea for noncompassionate government. Government by principle is the opposite of government by compassion; it is universalism rather than particularism; it is the "rule of law" rather than the "rule of man"; and it is modern rather than traditional. One cannot disagree with the need of government by principle, and fail to deplore too frequent departures from it, but one cannot imagine how this will bring compassionate government to the poor and the downtrodden. (Such is not Professor Lowi's objective.) Government by principle means decision by problem category rather than by the individual case.

I rather suspect that adherents of the "new political science" and the "new public administration" give a different interpretation to "government by principle." To this school of thought, all governmental decisions can be derived deductively from one or a few axiomatic philosophical principles, like those of the French Revolution, and especially that of "equality." Human life has this one dimension, equality, or at most a very few. Professor Michael Oakeshotte has argued that the politics of deduction from a few fixed principles is characteristic of immature and inexperienced people and that it has been the basic political mode in the last few hundred years, during which the masses have become increasingly involved in politics.[7] A study of large scale government decision making by emergency agencies staffed with all sorts of civilian amateurs showed their chief governing skill to be the ability to use a simplistic logic.[8] Leftist activism has found deductive politics advantageous. It is simple, easy to understand, and high in legitimacy; it has a broad mass appeal; and when it does not produce the desired result it can be junked unnoticed in favor of multidimensional social analysis. The following case illustrates these points.[9]

A few years ago a liberal Chicago lawyer lectured on the University of Illinois campus. He argued that certain areas of urban law should be reformed because they reflected middle class values and so failed to meet the needs of the black community. (What would reformers ever do without the "middle class"?) Note that he had already introduced the curious dichotomy of a unidimensional "middle class" (presumably all, or nearly all, white) and a multidimensional black community. He then urged the rejection of the "middle-class" notion that integration of neighborhoods must not be enforced. White communities, he went on, should be integrated forcibly by building public housing in them and requiring that a certain percentage of the residents in such housing be white. Should some of the whites in the community be tempted to move to the suburbs, he warned, then public housing would have to be built there, too. You may run and dodge, he declared, but we will follow you and put up a public housing project next door. Do not think you can escape us. (A Federal Judge so ordered in 1968, and public housing came to an end in the Chicago area.[10])

This was the usual first stage of analysis, where a policy is urged that is based only on a universal, abstract principle (in this case, as usual, equality). Mankind is unidimensional and human reality is like a machine, governed solely by a few universal principles. The only way to prevent segregation, he said, was to enforce integration (but by whom, against whom?).

The speaker moved into phase two of the procedure when he discussed zoning practices. These practices, he said, are based upon a few universal principles and do not recognize the multidimensionality of human society. Because, you see, zoning does not achieve his objective. It "classifies and segregates residents." Therefore, we must change it so that it recognizes the many rich dimensions of man and the wide variations among people along all of those dimensions. "The codes are written on middle class values and assume [that] all districts are the same, from the slums—to wealthy middle class residential areas." He urged that municipal codes be rewritten to meet the needs of every neighborhood; each nighborhood should be treated as if it were a municipality.

The objective of this man, though unstated, was clear enough. It was and is a value concern of many people. For those who do not believe that the end justifies the means, however, especially if the means include the sacrifice of one's intellectual integrity, a different form of intellectual analysis would appear to be necessary.[11] It would have to start with the multidimensionality of all people, and it could not assume the theme of equality as an absolute first principle, a priori (although this theme would be considered most seriously and would, in fact, be one of the principal subjects of debate).

Such an aproach would quickly resolve the discussion into one of distributions and the problem would become one of reconciling value conflicts arising in the course of discussing distributions. The resolution of such conflicts could only be in terms of trade-offs, compromises, bargaining, and never in terms of confronting absolute ethical principles as in the "politics of love," never in terms of "nonnegotiable demands." In this bargaining the claims of the "black community" (a stereotyped and ambiguous term) could be pressed very strongly and such abstract universals as moral equality would undoubtedly provide strong reinforcement for these value concerns. The moral abstractions would serve the purpose of helping to get a very high priority for these concerns.

In this form of argumentation, the absurdity, "the end justifies the means," would be strikingly absent; all men and institutions would be seen as multidimensional (complex) and would continue to be throughout the argument; the issues would be conflicts of values arising in discussions of distributions; and they would be resolved by a number of processes including bargaining, appeals to shared abstract moral principles, and analysis showing the proposed solution to be instrumental to a wider and more widely shared range of consequences (values) than had been at first supposed.

In the light of this analysis, recourse to the courts by activist reformers may be a mistake. Courts rule by deduction from general principles (in form at least: realists would argue that courts' decisions are psychological or ideological, their opinions being only and always rationalizations)[12] and lack the information and skill to rule in any other way. The only problem-solving training given to lawyers is in a tortured and conventionalized logic. At no time are they taught knowledge of consequences or introduced to the techniques that depend upon such knowledge, such as statistical decision theory. Decision by deduction-from-rules is the least compassionate kind there is. It also can result in self-defeating absurdities. For example, the recent spate of decisions to the effect that the 14th Amendment to the Constitution requires equal (per pupil) dollar expenditures on public education from district to district and hence outlaws reliance on property taxes could well have the effect, in a few cases at least, of requiring reduced per-pupil expenditures in the central city and increased expenditures in some suburbs. Money is only one of many things that go into the production of high-quality educational output. In Chicago, where the distribution of money to schools, on a per capita basis, is not determined by race but by such things as the stability or instability of neighborhoods, there are both mostly white and mostly black schools at the top of the list and also at the bottom. There, equalization of per-pupil expenditure means taking money (or the equivalent) from black schools and giving it to white ones (and vice versa).

The truth of Professor Oakeshotte's conclusions about the relation between inexperience and the use of deductive politics is becoming clearer all the time. Recently the Democratic Party, responding to the demand for participation in the political process by new and inexperienced categories of people, decided to make the party more representative by selecting women, blacks, and young people as delegates to its national nominating convention in roughly the same proportions as in the population at large. This change showed a profound misconception of the historical meaning of representation. The party was using the term in the statistical sense of a "representative sample," not in its historical political sense of speaking for some group or constituency as its delegate. Over the centuries, beginning in the church corporations and councils of the Middle Ages, the use of representatives of groups, rather than all members of the groups themselves, has been slowly developed and legitimized. Participation in church affairs became possible with the idea of church councils attended by representatives of churches, monasteries, and orders throughout Europe. The development of this process was a necessary step on the road to modern democracy.

In a speech before the New York Board of Rabbis, the Democratic candidate George McGovern "defended the imposition of quota-like standards for blacks, Latins, women and youth on delegations to the Democratic National Convention by saying that the purpose of a political convention was to provide representation for all groups making up the electorate."[13] Note, however, that these "groups" are not groups but demographic categories. Groups have organization or structure and so have and can formulate interests to be represented. Categories of people, on the other hand, have no interests and so cannot be represented. What are the "interests" of all or almost all 18-24 year olds? Of all or almost all women? On the other hand, note the interests of the League of Women Voters or the Students for a Democratic Society. These *are* groups and could send representatives to a convention to represent their interests. The candidate's hope of providing "representation for *all* groups making up the electorate" was pure fantasy, as I will demonstrate in the following pages. Apparently he meant categories, not groups. While the number of groups is finite, it is a hopelessly large number. The number of categories, however, is infinite.

The statistical use of the term "representative" is not, historically, a democratic concept. Russia claims that its Supreme Soviet (its "legislature") is the most representative legislative body in the world because it statistically represents the Russian people according to sex, age, occupation, location, etc. The Democratic Party will have to reform still further to be as representative as that; it is not yet a perfect random sample of the American people.

This historical distortion was carried out in the name of a simple principle, that of equality. It turns out that this principle is not simple at all, and that its complexities are beginning to open up like Pandora's Box. Everybody is equal to everybody else in some respect, and everybody is unequal to everybody else in some other respect. For example, we are all equally human beings, but we all have different (unequal) fingerprints (and hundreds of other qualities). Selecting the respect or criterion by reference to which we wish to use the term "equality" is not easy. It is not a task amendable to deductive logic, but only to a vast, uncodified experience.

Talcott Parsons lists five basic choices that an actor must make before the situation becomes sufficiently determinate for him to allow action, to allow him to even make a guess as to what to do. One of these choices is between a personal orientation and a collectivity orientation.[14] That is, the actor must decide whether the situation is one in which his responsibility is chiefly to himself or to others. This choice, however, is actually several choices. Toward which collectivity should the actor be oriented? There are many reference criteria that an individual could use to place himself in a category for one purpose or another, and these criteria have different qualities and hence different political implications. Tallness, for example, has not yet been chosen by many, but if it were, the category "tall people" would have a powerful case for discrimination (the denial of equality)—e.g., with regard to furniture size, door sizes, automobile size, etc.

Various overlooked groups are just starting to be heard from in various ways. One way is by letters to newspaper editors. For example, an Armenian writes: "My parents came to America after suffering through the first genocide of the 20th Century, when two-thirds of the Armenian population was massacred by the Turks. My father was always grateful to be in the United States and became a citizen. He and Armenians like him did not expect the government to provide for their families; instead they worked hard and provided and educated their own, never complaining. This is known as pride. Armenian was not taught in the schools when I was a student, much less heard of, but my brother, our friends and I managed to learn Armenian as well as English and received good educations."[15]

Or take this letter (exerpts) from a Hitler refugee who came to the United States from Austria in 1939.

> I am a first generation American, myself, but ever since arriving here as a Hitler refugee at the end of 1939, I have been incensed at the demands of some subsequent arrivals who think they have some special privileges due them on ethnic grounds.
>
> It was a hard beginning for us—but we worked hard and we were free. It would never have occurred to us to demand any special privileges because we had come from Austria.
>
> This is an English speaking country, with Spanish as the second language. (An Illinois law requires Spanish speaking teachers in some schools.) Children pick up English very quickly in school and there are adult evening classes to learn the language. Anyone who doesn't want to make this effort doesn't belong here. . . .[16]

Since many countries have language and regional differences, the

number of potential ethnic groups protesting discriminatory treatment runs into the hundreds, if not the thousands. As the associate
superintendent of the Oakland school system said: "It's not enough
just to have Chinese teachers . . . we have to have them qualified
to instruct in both Mandarin and Cantonese."[17]

Almost every nationality and race and tribe and interest association under the sun—literally thousands of them—have been "left
out" of the "new politics," with its reliance on a few simplistic
principles and a simplistic logic as substitutes for political wisdom.
Recently, in Chicago, an ex-convict, who spent eleven years in
prisons in Indiana and Wisconsin for safecracking and armed rob-
bery, announced plans to launch an ex-convicts' liberation movement.[18] I am told that a children's liberation movement is under-
way. The National Organization for Women has a male "Task
Force on the Masculine Mystique" that demonstrates against men
having to be successful.[19]

Or how about "good looks" as a criterion for interpreting equality and hence alleging discrimination? The *Wall Street Journal* has
reported that business firms generally discriminate in favor of good
looks on the part of both male and female employees. An enter-
prising newspaper took an informal survey to find out whether, in
this year of the "new politics" (1972), the crop of Democratic
presidential candidates practiced "looks discrimination" in their
campaign office hiring and promotions: " . . . the consensus was
that a pretty face and a bouncy figure will help a girl get the job."
The rule in Representative Shirley Chisholm's office seemed to be:
"If you have three applicants for a job and all three are equally
qualified, the most attractive will probably get the job." In Senator
McGovern's office: " . . . all other things being equal, looks helps.
It's the same as private industry."[20] Here is, obviously, the basis in
"repression" for a new and different kind of liberation movement.
The possibilities it opens up are both flabbergasting and frightening
(e.g., the distribution of IQs, athletic prowess, beauty, etc.). A recent survey showed a strong negative relation between obesity and
promotion.[21]

Why has our politics not been plagued by a plethora of such demands for representation or "liberation"? Because of historical
factors and processes too subtle for politically inexperienced minds

to grasp. Among the skills of competent thinking is the ability to make distinctions. Each distinction represents a new class of phenomena to be treated differently. Good thinkers deal with a very large number of classes, which is to say that good thinking is complex. Experts deal with complexity. Inexperienced people—and the new groups in politics are politically inexperienced—must simplify in order to gain any cognitive grasp at all. This need to simplify makes them politically dangerous, which is to say, likely to make wrong decisions.

Political events, at least in a democracy's domestic politics, are largely concerned with distributive problems (who benefits and who pays?), and so the choice of reference criteria, hence groups, is basic to the political process. It determines whether one feels discriminated against. Depending upon how this choice is made, ordinary and even routine administrative decisions may well provoke violent political action. Thus, a regulation setting minimum height limits for policemen in Guyana caused bloody riots.[22] A few years ago the relocation of one part of a university (the French-speaking part) brought about the downfall of a Belgian government. Recently, Vincent T. Ximenes, the Mexican-American member of the Equal Employment Opportunity Commission, complained that Michigan's minimum height regulation for state troopers—5'9"—discriminated against Mexican-Americans, whose average height is alleged to be 5'6". If the latter figure were used, it would "discriminate" against Chinese-Americans, whose average height is alleged to be 5'1½".[23] It would certainly discriminate against women and, still more disquieting, it would discriminate against a "group" that has not yet surfaced—short people. The Florida attorney general recently stated his belief that height and weight requirements of any kind violate the equal-protection clause of the Constitution.[24]

An interesting illustration is the case of Sanshiro Miyamoto of Detroit. He has a burning desire to be a policeman but the Detroit Department's minimum height standard is 5'7", while Mr. Miyamoto is only 5'5". He "has stretched himself to 5'6½" through efforts that included having his wife hit him on the head to raise a bump." He was still rejected. Police Commissioner John F. Nichols made this statement: "Mr. Miyamota might make a very fine policeman, and we'd be happy to have him on the force. However, we can't change a rule for him without doing it for everyone. He still must come up to our standards."[25] In other words, compassion for Mr. Miyamoto would be discrimination for all-others-below-5'7"-who-wanted-to-be-policemen—a possible reference group. Or is this case just an example of the sociological argument that functionaries cannot deal with substantive rationality? It certainly is an example of universalism (even-handed justice) versus particularism. Universalism is generally considered to be a distinguishing and valued quality of modern administration. The perception of height limitations as discrimination is now spreading to other states and localities.

The generation of reference groups and categories to claim special privilege (by alleging discrimination) has a quality of feeding upon itself that systems engineers would call deviation amplifying (or positive) feedback. The generation of some groups or categories stimulates the generation of still more, etc., as the special position achieved by some people reminds others that they may do the same. "Indeed, many of the strongest advocates of 'equal opportunity' and 'affirmative action' are finding it increasingly difficult to implement their new policies without exacerbating resistance by those who feel that special treatment and open enrollment and quotas are designed only for certain segments of the population."[26] Chinese-American parents in San Francisco, for instance, brought suit charging discrimination because San Francisco schools do not provide Chinese-speaking teachers. The suit reached the Supreme Court in the fall term, 1973.[27] In Oakland, "Chicano, Portuguese, Chinese, Spanish, Anglo-Saxon and black parent organizations all are clamoring for special recognition in the schools." These complexities, along with others, resulted eventually in the murder of the superintendent.[28]

Some reactions are probably intended to ridicule the claims to special treatment, such as the newly formed LATER—the Left-handed Alliance Toward Equal Rights—whose action program demands college courses in left-handed studies, immortalizing such lefties as Julius Caesar, Charlemagne, and Babe Ruth, and that ten percent of all advertising show models in left-handed poses. More serious—in fact, deadly serious—is the growth of ethnic group consciousness, sense of outrage, and feelings of discrimination.[29] In August, 1972, six national Jewish organizations sent HEW a letter detailing a number of specific cases "where affirmative action programs, designed to promote hiring of minorities and women, had resulted in discrimination against white males." They were particularly concerned with a federal regulation that said: "Neither minority nor female employees should be required to possess higher qualifications than those of the lowest qualified incumbent." They received no satisfaction from HEW even when, after six months, they sent a follow-up letter to HEW's ombudsman for reverse discrimination [sic].[30]

The oversimplification of deductive politics has another disturbing implication. The fractionalization of our political consensus implied in this simplistic, inexperienced approach to political action presages a regression in our administrative practices, as the above cases illustrate. The gradual, painful, and only partial separation of administration from the political process, a separation that has allowed us to develop administrative norms of achievement and universalism (equality before the law) and hence efficient and impartial administration, is in danger of being reversed.

Raids on administrative resources for political reasons are becoming increasingly common at all levels of government and in private organizations, as well. I will cite two examples which suggest the dumping of achievement norms in favor of hiring on an infinitely expansible ascriptive basis. Eleanor Hicks, a twenty-nine-year-old black female, six years out of college and with six years experience in the U.S. Foreign Service, mostly in Bangkok, Thailand, was appointed in July, 1972, to be United States consul in Nice, on the French Riviera, certainly one of the choicest berths available. Ms. Hicks "acknowledged in an interview that the job may have come to her because she is a minority group triple threat (under thirty, black, female) at a time when such credentials help."[31] The administrative harm done by such ascriptive appointments could not possibly be compensated by the miniscule political brownie points they are believed to win.

In many colleges today, academic appointments are based on ascriptive criteria, again in the hope of political gain (this time in the form of a continued flow of dollars from Washington): "Under pressure from HEW, a growing number of universities are giving preference, and sometimes exclusive consideration, in faculty hiring to blacks and to women."[32] (As of the summer of 1972, the federal government had brought charges of sex discrimination against more than 350 institutions of higher education that receive federal money.) The writer of this letter to *The American Sociologist* had a glimpse, if only a restricted one, of the possibilities of allowing such political raids on administrative institutions in an age of mass, inexperienced, politics: "Besides being unfair, a policy of reverse discrimination opens a Pandora's Box from which may flow untold evil and turmoil. If we must select new faculty (or students or those to be promoted) on the basis of race or sex, why not on the basis of religion or membership in an ethnic group? Surely Catholics are under-represented in sociology departments. How about Poles? Those with Spanish surnames? Italians? Are there not too many Jews? How much weight should various ascribed characteristics be given? For what rewards? The list of such questions is almost endless and the questions are not trivial."[33]

Extensive reverse discrimination in hiring in sociology departments in favor of women and minorities has recently been documented—and fortunately by a woman. The most common reason for this practice is pressure and commands from college and university administrators anxious to keep the federal dollars flowing by meeting HEW guidelines, which are clearly inconsistent with the Civil Rights Act of 1964.[34] When academic administrators plead with HEW bureaucrats to tell them how to comply without violating the law, to tell them what they must do to combine ascription (the "guidelines") with achievement (the Civil Rights Act), the bureaucrats have no suggestions to make. They do not know how to do it either.[35] Jewish groups are particularly, and understandably, fearful of this most recent version of the QUOTA.

In Dayton, Ohio, a group of seventeen white policemen have sued the city for $1.5 million, charging racial discrimination in promotions. A promotional list they were on by examination had been allowed to expire while the city followed a policy of promoting only blacks. A court ruled this promotional policy illegal in the spring of 1973, and the seventeen brought suit.[36] Despite the court ruling, other cities have been forced by HEW and the United States

Department of Justice to adopt the same promotion policy, at least temporarily. (As a result, the Chicago Police Department had over 600 vacancies in the summer of 1974.)

Because federal officials insist that school districts must equalize spending between schools to qualify for federal aid, teachers are recruited and added to schools without any justification in educational administration. Chicago made 182 such placements in 1971-72.[37] Numbers, like machines, are stupid. Why should not someone insist on an equal per-student expenditure in the universities as between liberal arts and humanities students, on one side, and science and engineering and medical students, on the other? Where can it end?

The questions are indeed "almost endless," and they are certainly "not trivial." Society—its institutions and practices, its people—is the immensely complex result of a very long history. It is multi-dimensional, not one-dimensional. The principle of equality will not govern a nation. Let us hope that political experience and wisdom are acquired soon by the new forces that have been unleashed.[38]

To that end, I shall now try to suggest some of the immense complexity involved in selecting reference criteria for the purpose of giving operational meaning to the "simple" principle of equality. Reference criteria are elements that go into an individual's subjective identity. They answer the question: Who am I? The answer provides the individual his collectivity orientations. A list of the more important criteria that might be chosen would include occupation, sex, age, race, religion, nationality, political ideology, socio-economic class, political party. Another list of lesser criteria, probably in order of declining importance, would include physical handicaps, educational level, marital status, family role, geographical location, divorce status, height, weight, looks. All of these, and others, could be further subdivided to expand our list of criteria indefinitely, for example, six-year old, seven-year old,[39] etc.; or high school freshman, high school junior, . . . Ph.D., etc.

Which criteria are chosen and why? Do the choices vary from one problem situation to another (giving us changeable personalities), or are they relatively stable (giving some credence to personality theory)? Do the choices change over time: are they related to age or experience? Are they the result, probably accidental, of a person's position in some communication structure (which determines what cues reach him)? Or are the choices the result of the individual's purposive or accidental primary and/or secondary affiliations?

Some of the criteria, clearly, are fixed; many others seem to be variable. Stable criteria would include sex, race, nationality, and some physical qualities. Variable criteria would or might include age, class, politics, religion, and occupation. For the variable criteria there are different degrees of variability, from high (e.g., age) to low (e.g., religion, occupation), and the degree of variability may change over time. For example, occupation was a more variable criterion in an age of low information, when work was defined on the job rather than in preentry institutions such as professional and trade schools. Labor used to be a flexible commodity; it is fast becoming fixed capital. The criteria of political partisanship, marital status, and religion may also be more variable today than in the past. For example, groups of divorced men organized to protest the treatment they have received from courts are very modern phenomena. An example is Fathers United For Equal Rights, a Maryland group with over 350 members (as of the summer of 1972), which has challenged Maryland divorce laws on the constitutional ground that they deny men the equal protection of the laws. Other states also have such groups. The Maryland group has an interesting auxiliary called Second Wives Coalition, composed of women who have married divorced men and are suffering because they feel that their husbands are being wrung dry financially.

We know little about what stimulates such reference choices.[40] It may be a public policy or personality to which one must react; or existing distributions may be brought to one's attention in any of many ways—distributions to which one must react (i.e., choose sides; "stand up and be counted"). If one is told by an aspiring politician (a person without power who wants it) that we spend more on lipstick than on cancer research (and we always spend more on *some* thing than on something else), does one not have to react to this piece of information?[41] Or the individual may belong to a primary or secondary group in which adherence to a selected list of reference criteria is part of the price of membership. To be a political scientist or a sociologist nowadays, for example, one almost has to be a Democrat. To be young, it helps to belong to the category of people who say that American participation in the Vietnam War was immoral. To be a delegate at the 1972 Democratic National Convention, one had to endorse the lettuce boycott.

The groups to which we aspire to belong will probably have divided the world into the good guys and the bad guys, which means that they provide us with a list of reference criteria that we must choose and a list that we must not choose (the "enemies"). Occasionally, a reference criterion must be chosen in response to some expressive stimuli—words or gestures (e.g., "fascist pig"). Different combinations of criteria, variability and degrees of variability could produce a very large variety of politics.

In the modern industrial society, achievement criteria are the most important and these, for most people, relate to occupations. Achievement criteria, like specialization, have a social-evaluation dimension. Achievement means not only to accomplish by one's own efforts, but to accomplish something of social value. To some extent, poverty is an achieved status (though not, of course, if it results from racial discrimination, which is an ascription process), but it has not in the past been an achievement of high social value (and I very much doubt that current efforts to give it social respectability will be very successful). Interest associations are largely achievement groups and power is distributed to such groups, especially occupational groups and especially if the occupation has high social evaluation.

Achieved roles probably generate more value consciousness, more ideology, than ascribed ones. It would seem that achievement would involve more investment of the self, more affect, more value. The more easily the occupational skill is acquired and the less time the role is maintained by the individual—that is, the less skilled and the more changeable the work—the less investment would the individual have in the role and the less value it would have for him. Consequently, it would provide a much weaker reference criterion than its opposite—say, a professional role.

Structural units, such as parts of an organization, can only create small and hence politically insignificant reference groups. Likewise, social status (class) has been so weakened in the modern industrial society that it no longer generates politically strong reference groups (class conflict).

Transient, low-value, low-skill roles are often reified for the purpose of giving some solidity to what is essentially an ephemeral stage or period in a person's life. For example, the president of an equal-rights-for-women group, writing to the newspaper in support of the lettuce boycott, said: "Farm workers are perhaps the most deprived members of our affluent society. They live in poor housing, on limited incomes, have limited educational opportunities, and limited or no medical care." The reader feels a bit puzzled with such a statement. The reason is that the writer implies that an achieved status is ascribed, or, as I put it earlier, reifies a temporary stage in a person's life. During a recent six-year period 45 percent of the American people had at some point been in the poverty category, according to a University of Michigan survey. The reason that many people feel somewhat outraged when college students apply for food stamps is that they have a sense, however vague, of the distinction between ascribed and achieved poverty.

"Revisionist" social scientists are becoming an interesting source of political reference groups. Something curious is going on at the "forefront" of social science, where we find the "new political science," the "new public administration," and their counterparts in sociology and psychology. The positivist distinction between fact and value is being inverted. Many members of the social-science avant garde, while insisting on the value-laden and subjective nature of the "old" social science (and all other sciences), demand an objective status for their political (and other) evaluations. Protestors and demonstrators, such as campus demonstrators of the past few years, are automatically justified on the ground that "if they protest, they have something to protest about."[42]

Some of these social scientists take the position that there is no malefaction or delinquency in society; it is all a matter of society *calling* some perfectly ordinary people malefactors or delinquents. "Objectively," the story goes, so-called malefaction is just "behavior"; the prosecution or punishment of such behavior is a value-laden, reprehensible malefaction by "society." They give this position a touch of legitimacy with a bit of "scientific" jargon, calling it "labeling theory." "Recent theoretical developments have emphasized that *delinquency is an assembling production by officials* far more than it is a behavior pattern of young people (or old people) and that, moreover, the latter cannot possibly be separated from the former." As for older social science, it is "an arbitrary and imperialistic extension of the sociologist's mentality, growing largely out of concerns implanted and supported by agents and agencies of social control." It has even been claimed that schizophrenia is largely a creation of labelers.[43]

Why the delinquent's behavior should be any more "natural" and "value free" than the officials' or the older sociologists' behavior is not explained. The "theory" explains the behavior of those labeled but not that of the labelers themselves. Therefore, why the former should be natural and the latter reprehensible and value laden is impossible to understand except as an expression of preferences. It is true, of course, that behavior in "nature" is just behavior and that the adjectives "good," "bad," etc., are attached to it within societies by comparing the behavior with social codes. Thus, evaluation is conventional and relative to cultural norms. Absolute good and evil are not scientifically comprehensible ideas. That "new" social scientists have only recently rediscovered this very obvious fact is one of the many puzzling phenomena of this puzzling age.

The most common activating stimuli of politics are the comparative percentages of groups—not facts like hunger, unemployment, etc., but the relative percentages of groups that are hungry, unemployed, etc. Statistical distributions between groups (more often categories; a group has social structure) are the principal political facts, the principal political objectives. The key to this simplistic politics is, hence, the reference criteria by which the groups are defined. They determine the lines of battle. By virtue of this choice, inequality that was not apparent before suddenly becomes apparent.

Stable criteria are more likely to be ascriptive (that is, related to who you are rather than to what you have become, or to what you can do). Variable criteria are more likely to be achievement related. (I say "more likely" because there are criteria, such as age, that are both variable and ascriptive.) The old liberal, pluralistic politics, with its interest associations, based so largely on the vari-

able criterion of occupational interests, was a politics of achievement. People earned (or "slugged") their way to the "top." The
new "politics of love" is largely a politics of ascription. Demands
issue from who you are, not from what you have achieved. The
criteria for selection to the Democratic National Convention were
mostly ascriptive: age, sex, and race. Joe Smith helps select a presidential candidate because he is eighteen, not because he has earned
the right to do so.

Thus far I have tried to show that using a principle such as
equality in making political choices is difficult because of the
difficulty of fixing on the groups by reference to which equality is
to be assessed. It is not enough merely to determine a criterion for
selecting a group (often really a category); the attribute or quality
whose percentage distribution between the chosen groups is to be
compared must also be determined. The chosen group, as defined
by the reference criterion, may have a low percentage of one attribute relative to the other group(s) but a high percentage of another
attribute. The result is that a case for discrimination (inequality)
can be made for one attribute but not for the other. Women, for
example, hold a low percentage of corporate presidencies compared with men, but they average seven and a half more years of
life.[44] On the latter attribute, then, it is men who are "discriminated
against." The principle of equality will be of little help in deciding
which of the two discriminations is the greater. Furthermore, while
a smaller percentage of American women than American men are
corporation presidents, perhaps the percentage is larger than the
percentage of Arabian men or black men who are corporation
presidents. The case for discrimination, therefore, the political
struggle for greater benefits and power, requires both the careful
choice of reference criteria defining the groups to be compared and
a careful choice of the attribute whose distribution between the
groups is to be compared.

I suggested above a possible case for discrimination against tall
men as a group, using such attributes as furniture and door sizes.
On other attributes, however, tall men may fare very well:

> A survey of 1970 Pitt business school graduates found those
> over six feet commanded a starting salary in their first jobs
> 10 per cent higher than those under six feet. A similar survey in

1967 had shown a four per cent advantage for the taller applicants.
. . . So now there is a new obstacle for all but a few job applicants to overcome. Height discrimination.
But it averages out. The six-footers are only getting even for
the short beds they have to sleep in, and the low profile cars they
have to drive.[45]

As with other values, the ordinal position of any attribute in a
value scheme or preference ordering changes over time. Virginity,
for example, once a highly valued attribute, has now sunk so low
that Art Buchwald humorously suggests the need for a Virgin's
Anti-Defamation League.

Because of its political potency, statistical comparison becomes
an important tool in the play of power. Although the former head
of the Equal Employment Opportunity Commission, Mr. Clifford
Alexander, has said that "comparisons are not the way to improve
the basic positions of blacks,"[46] the comparison of percentage distributions is how these "basic positions" are defined, and that is
how, therefore, they will be improved. Absolute values on the attributes will not be advantageous. There are many more unemployed
whites than unemployed blacks. The same is probably true for most
conceivable attributes. If compassion were the heart of the problem,
absolute numbers would be the relevant ones. The use of percentage
distributions shows that the heart of the problem is politics, not
compassion. As Rep. Martha Griffiths said, "What we're really
talking about in ERA [Equal Rights Amendment] is money. Who
pays and who gets."[47]

If reference criteria, in postindustrial society, at least, are as
complex and variable as I have tried to suggest, a people cannot be
usefully defined for political purposes by statistical distributions.
What we describe or define today will not be the same thing tomorrow. What, for example, is still left of the distributions of political-
behavior research of the past ten years or so?

Asking this question raises a still more perplexing problem for
reference-group selection and hence for public-policy making. We
define reference categories in snapshot, cross-sectional terms such
as young, old, student, etc. These categories, however, are only
stages in an individual's lifetime. If we took a life-span perspective
we would organize people into cohorts—into groups born about

the same time. Such cohorts would go together through the various highs and lows of life, its triumphs and its tragedies, its ups and downs, its many roles. The categories we presently use, being temporary stages, would tend to disappear. Thus "the poor," "the student," etc., would tend to disappear. They would refer not to kinds of people but to kinds of stages in a life span.[48] They would consequently be much less suitable reference criteria for policy making. Public-policy thinking would be pointed in different directions. Public policy, hence, would be different. It might not be better or worse, but it would be different. National health insurance would suggest itself before Medicare. Lifetime concerns such as consumerism might get a bigger play. Political power, however, is distributed chiefly according to occupational-achievement criteria and the reference groups that arise from them. Consequently, policy making according to a life-span perspective is hardly feasible. Such a perspective does suggest, however, a parallel world of policy, of political concerns, of equity definitions and perceptions of discrimination. There is nothing absolute about current political claims, concepts, perceptions, and values. Decision making by means of deductions from absolute ethical principles is a bemusing illusion.

A population should be defined in terms of its more enduring features—in terms of its institutions. It is the political institutions, I submit, and the politicians and voters who understand them, that have contained the possible variations and complexities outlined above and thus made politics comprehensible and reasonably calculable. One implication of this suggestion is that a population in the midst of revolution has no features: it does not yet exist. It is a mass of potential, and that is all it is. The supreme horror of revolution is the almost total loss of identity of a whole population, and its corrolary, the loss of individual identities.[49] Another implication is that perhaps political scientists should take a second hard look at behavioralism. Behavioralism is the political scientist's contribution to the ascriptive regression of these bewildering years because it is reductionist and hence unable to deal adequately with institutions.[50] Furthermore, behavioralism has quite generally been interpreted as statisticizing and so has contributed to the numbers game of modern politics that I have been describing.

10 SOLUTIONS

Changing Personalities, Changing Organizations

This account will by now have impressed the reader as hopelessly pessimistic. Actually, the reality of the situation is not so bad as it appears. The fact is, most people do not suffer unduly at the hands of the large, modern bureaucratic organization. Human institutions are shaped by the kind of human material available to them.[1] Before industrialization can begin, there must appear some industrial men—some men and women who can imagine themselves in different and better circumstances, as rich persons, proprietors, doctors, teachers, or whatever "better" role is available.

They must also be socially mobile, that is, members of social institutions that will allow them to do something about these dreams. Membership in a large family, which puts loyalty to kinsman above everything, is a hopeless prospect for a young businessman. His family obligations to hire and support and finance kinsmen make it impossible for him to get ahead or even to stay even.

He must also be able to move geographically, both to avoid kinsmen and to find and move to new opportunities. As Daniel Lerner says, he must have geographical, social, and psychological mobility—he must be able to change places, social positions, and personalities. And he must be motivated to want to do these things. Thus, industrialism arises apace with industrial man.[2]

One of the greatest enemies of industrialism is the extended family (very large ones are called tribes). As the size and functions of the family decrease, creating a new type of man, industrial organizations increase. As technology has decreed the ever larger, more abstract, more impersonal, more expert, less compassionate kind of organization, the kind of childhood experiences ("socialization") that would make membership in such organizations unbearably painful has declined proportionately. We have the large impersonal bureaucracy, among other reasons, because the socialization that most people experience renders it, if not painless, at least tolerable. As Arthur Stinchcombe says: "The organizational inventions that can be made at a particular time in history depend on the social technology at the time."[3]

To the extent that many people suffer either "in" our modern organizations or in dealing with them as clients, consumers, etc., we have a gap between the socialization of the individual and the technology of organization design—between the person and the institution. I feel rather strongly that this gap will be narrowed, if at all, not by gimmicks of the kind discussed in preceding chapters but by further evolution of the socialization process and further development of organization design—by evolving personalities and organization structures. The truly determining elements of the problem are changing families, socialization practices, motivations, personal orientations, and work, and the growing importance of creativity relative to productivity.

In societies changing from traditional to modern ways there is a period when both sets of behaviorial rules, the old and the new, are contradicting one another. Neither is able to exercise much control. Anomie, individual normlessness, leads to disorganization of social institutions. Suicide and crime increase. Personal opportunism increases as each individual discovers that he can find a semilegitimate rule to justify just about anything. This situation leads to highly personalized behavior in government—to what we would call graft, corruption, bribery, nepotism, amicism, and worse.[4]

Individuals oscillate between new and old practices and find satisfaction in neither. New practices are copied and formally promulgated without being undrstood, while affairs are actually governed by older norms and relationships. Thus, a formal civil-service system will only serve to hide somewhat an out-and-out system of nepotism or tribal favoritism. Dual pricing is endemic, the price serving both a modern economic function and an older, perhaps kinship or gift-giving, one.

Government is distrusted quite generally, and most people believe that you have to have "pull" or have to pay a bribe to get even the most elementary right honored by bureaucrats.[5] As for the "freed" peasant masses, they migrate, lonely and alienated, to the cities, where they reconstruct a social system along the lines of communes of fellow tribesmen, while the old folks, also lonely, stay on the farm, gradually becoming too weak to work it.

This description, while reasonably accurate, was designed to suggest a parallel with many young people in the advanced industrial societies (what some people are beginning to call postindustrial society). The breakup of the family is seen in the apparently growing rejection of parental rules and values from a fairly young age (fifteen or sixteen). We now have over a million runaways a year. A new set of personal behavior norms has not yet been constructed, though an antibourgeois youth culture is rapidly in the making, aided by the instant communication of the media.

As of yet, neither set of norms is working well; one has been rejected and the other is not yet complete or adequate and perhaps also not fully accepted. The result is a great increase in individualism and in personal opportunism in regard to organizations, and, I believe, interpersonal relations in general: take all you can get and give no more than you have to. There is a general antiorganization ("antiestablishment") feeling, something approaching philosophical anarchy, that many young people have embraced without exploring its implications. Many refuse to work for most organizations, regarded as part of the "establishment," both in government and industry. To do so would be to "cop out."

For some, even more virulent destructive attacks against the old society and its "establishment" have been necessary, including bombing and sabotage. Still others set their face against the present (new) society by digging out old clothing and hair styles, old farming methods (organic), and old industry—weaving, candlemaking, small farming. Communes of young men and women replace families for awhile, and "relevant" educational courses are taught by the young themselves, since the old establishment is "incapable of change."

Why is the youth movement for the moment almost worldwide? (Fidel Castro has just revealed that in Cuba 25 percent of school-age children have dropped out and only 25 percent are at their proper grade level.) Because polynormativism (competing codes) is for the moment almost worldwide. To fall between two codes of personal conduct is to be subject to forces that are independent of the content of the codes. Polynormativism is, however, a transient condition, a sort of "changing of the guard."

As was noted in the previous chapter, among the various decisions an individual must make about a situation before he has defined it well enough to take action with regard to it is whether the situation calls for an individual, personal orientation, or for a collective one—whether the situation calls for him to act on his own behalf or on behalf of a collectivity. In the modern period, the individual needs to be socialized to adopt the collective orientation in all his dealings with economic and governmental organizations (actually, with "bureaucratic" organizations). This orientation is little more than the golden-rule "norm" extended to nonprimary organizations: do unto others as you would have them do unto you, or, in Kant's terms, so act that your actions could be generalized into universal law. Actually, the golden rule is our modern administrative norm of equal treatment, the norm of universalism.

Many primary, solidarity-group experiences are consistent with this norm—for example, investing one's affect in the goals and contributions of the other group members (or, as the psychologists would say, "cathecting" their goals and contributions). Such small-group experiences reinforce a collectivity orientation. At the same time, it is in the small group that we learn to expect special treatment and acquire the belief that someone has the power to give it.

The argument that, if X violates a norm, there will be a noticeable increase in violations of that norm is not convincing. In that form, in fact, it is simply not true. A collective orientation will probably not be created by rational argument. Indeed, it is likely that individual rationality experiences reinforce the personal, noncollective orientations. It is usually true that stealing works better for the individual in a society in which there is little theft, that cheating works best for the individual in classes in which there is little cheating, etc.

Individualism results from reinforcing experiences where deviancy is not punished. The "son-of-a-bitch" comes out ahead because the rest will not compete on his level. Our courts—as usual, a generation behind the public—have been handing down the kind of decisions in the 1960s and 1970s that parents handed down in the 1940s and 1950s. Although this decisional orientation will change, it hasn't yet, and in March, 1972, the Supreme Court ruled, five to two, that using obscene and threatening language to a policeman is protected by the Constitution—one more in a long line of decisions reinforcing deviancy and encouraging a personal rather than a collective orientation toward our institutions.

In child training, the origin of this reinforced individualism is "over-security"—where the child is not required to pay a price for his love. The "permissive" child rearing of the past twenty-five years has been discredited and many parents have discarded it. (Even Dr. Benjamin Spock has discarded it.) Corresponding social doctrines denying individual responsibility—psychiatric forgiveness, the responsibility of society, and other denials of individual freedom—are now under attack from many quarters and may have about run their course. Excesses produce their own counterforces. Note the growing antipathy to "coddling criminals."[6] These changes, assuming that they are indeed occurring, all make easier the inculcation of the collective-orientation norm, namely: *you* should not get an exception (favor) because the social value of the administrative action is more important than its cost to you personally.

The continuing belief in favors—the belief that there is someone who can grant them and that it is all right to get them—depresses the collective orientation. The belief in favors is incompatible with the Kantian imperative, the golden rule, and the modern administrative norm, i.e., that everyone in the same problem category is to be treated alike. If I have the power to grant favors, I obviously believe in them and cannot truthfully say to a suppliant, "If I grant you an exception I will have to do the same for everyone else who is similarly situated."

Modern man needs to learn to be comfortable with impersonality. All this amounts to is giving a high value to instrumentalism, to the achievement of established goals. Personalism *versus* impersonality is similar to group maintenance *versus* group goal achievement. Group maintenance is largely an affective and personal process. Group maintenance is less important today with our immense stock of standardized, interchangeable roles; our great geographical, social, and organizational mobility; our reduced interpersonal expectations; our segregation of affective needs in increased leisure and related opportunities and institutions (groups, hobbies, vacations, associations, play, etc.).

One would also expect a heightened instrumentalism to be associated with a longer time sense, with the ability to defer gratification (which is a good psychological definition of capitalism). Waiting for organizational action should, therefore, become less painful. In the normal course of maturation people acquire an increased ability to wait for gratifications. We would expect socialization processes to be more effective in this respect than they have been in the past.

The family is changing and so is the kind of socialization of which it is capable. Specifically, parental roles are changing, and especially the role of the wife-mother. Alternatives to the mother role are growing, as is the disinclination for women to assume it. More and more women are refusing to "sacrifice" themselves for children. They demand work equality with men, "unisex," women's liberation, smaller families. As the director of the Women's Bureau recently reminded other women, jobs today "aren't men's jobs. Technology has made them anybody's jobs."

The kibbutzim of Israel provide the most striking example of this change, the women having rejected motherhood for work equality and comradeship with men. When the children of the kibbutz reach the organization, the latter will change regardless of any managerial philosophies or strategies. Of course, I do not expect mankind to lose his social needs—his needs for interpersonal affect, security, and reinforcement. But what satisfies these needs will change. I expect abstract systems (impersonal systems of rules; artificial systems) to become more acceptable. They will be the source of more reinforcements, comparatively, than the favors of families and other natural systems.

Much has been said about the growing "professionalization" of work, and so I need not dwell upon this factor at length. Professionalized work is associated with personal responsibility for both defining and solving problems; interorganizational mobility; peer evaluations rather than the bureaucratic, hierarchical kind; motivation through professional growth, work itself, and problem challenge, rather than the actual or symbolical achievement of power and status in a sort of Maslowian primitivism. Such changes must be matched by changes in organizations—in the uses of authority, in hierarchy and communication, in incentive systems, and in many other aspects of organization life.

Incentive systems within our bureaucratic organizations have been based on the assumption that man's central needs were for security and prestige (esteem of self and others). Thus, by doling out or withholding money and status, the discipline needed by our technologies could be obtained. There is growing evidence that a long period of affluence has weakened these needs and thereby decreased their utility as incentives. Expressive, self-actualizing kinds of needs are becoming dominant.[7] This change, too, suggests changes in organization structure and practices in the same directions suggested by the professionalizing (or at least upgrading) of work.

We are approaching a surplus of means in relation to ends (if we have not indeed reached that stage already), a condition that suggests an emphasis on creativity and innovation rather than production—an emphasis on the discovery of new uses for our resources rather than on their careful husbanding. This statement is supported by the fact that we sell abroad ten times as much technology as we purchase from abroad. Innovation needs, in turn, suggest the growth of smaller organizations, of temporary organizations, of the use of limited project teams—in general, the increased use of small, temporary, nonroutinized, interdisciplinary arrangements of various kinds. This development fits the growing automation of the functions of the large production-oriented bureaucracy, first the mechanical ones and now increasingly the decisional and communication ones. As people are displaced from programmed and automated manufacturing industry they become available for a great increase in service industry, which is not so easily programmed, and which is amenable to much smaller organization units.

Perhaps I can summarize these last few pages by saying that as individuals change in our changing culture and feel less strongly the need for an organization to be like a family, more and more people will work in more and more organizations that are in some ways more like families. Man and his institutions will fit one another better. A perfect fit we can never expect, short of genetic or behavioral engineering. Such engineering is a long way off. We have not yet decided how to select either the engineers or the designs.

For quite some time, a number of psychologically oriented students of our bureaucratic organizations have regarded them as unfit places for adults to work in. (See, for example, the works of Chris Argyris.) The reader may very well wonder why we should do any better in the future than we have done in the past. The answer, I think, is that our primitive technology determined the kinds of organizations we needed. Organizations with dull, routinized, highly scheduled work, and functioning in a world having an excess of needs over resources, needed strong controls, strong discipline, and centralized top-down planning. Now, however, technology has advanced tremendously and may, therefore, no longer be so controlling. Hence other factors that I have listed, freed somewhat from technological constraints, will have more power to shape man and his organizations. It is inconceivable that some cosmic perversity will maintain or even widen the gap between man and his institutions. I expect it to narrow, however, unless man heeds the siren cries of false prophets (of which there are always many) and follows them into slavery.

The most potent threat is the growing efficiency of administrative information and control systems. In this there is real danger to the individual. Up to now, administrative inefficiency with regard to information processing has had the benign effect of dividing our lives into almost autonomous compartments. Events in one compartment—say, kicking the dog at home—do not affect outcomes in another—say, promotion at work.[8] Within organizations, this administrative inefficiency with regard to information processing results, as Chester Barnard said, in departmentalization.[9] Pyramidal, hierarchial lines of authority act as a communications network, the executive positions therein as switchboards. Communication within the departmentalized organization, and hence coordination and control, takes place by means of telephone and face-to-face conversations, memoranda, interdepartmental meetings.

Such communication depends somewhat on the cooperation of individuals and solidarity groups ("cliques"). They have something to exchange, namely, their cooperation. In these circumstances, they can strike informal bargains and in this way protect individual interests and needs.

The perfection of data-processing technique may eliminate this means of individual protection.[10] Control systems may approach perfection. The compartmentalization of life and the departmentalization of the organization may break down. Information about events in one compartment may be the more likely to show up in another. Backstage areas with their performance-spoiling information may disappear. As everyone is plugged into an automated information system, interdepartmental cooperation with regard to information flow within organizations may be less and less necessary. If all these things transpire, we will come closer and closer to the frightful day that Orwell wrote about, when each of us will be "front and center" at all times.[11] Should all these developments continue to completion, the needs and methods of the large bureaucratic organization would become triumphant and the last possibility of administrative compassion would disappear. Orwell would be seen as a prophet rather than as a storyteller, and we would discover that our freedoms had resulted not from the philosophies of Milton and Mill but from administrative inefficiency.

Although this "new management science" has already been used in some areas in which coordination, control, and speed of decision are crucial, as in the Air Force's SAGE (Semi-Automatic Ground Environment) air-defense system, its proponents often complain of resistance from [illiterate] "humanists." The "new science" has not spread greatly. In many places its promise has proved to be a false one, as, for example, in the use of Planning, Programming, Budgeting (PPB) as a device for achieving greater rationality in government decisions.[12] PPB has been almost a total failure and has been dropped by state governments almost as fast as it was adopted after 1965 when President Lyndon Johnson ordered it installed throughout the federal government. Although long abandoned in fact, it was formally dropped by Washington only in 1971. (By the way, who is *responsible* for the billions of dollars and millions of man-hours wasted on this gimmick? It all could have been saved if we had had more heroic resisters to "innovation.")[13]

The new management-science developments have not been widely adopted because the needs of the time are for more creativity rather than for more rationality, coordination, and control. As our business colleges blindly develop and turn out more and more control science and control scientists—experts in a mathematically demonstrated rationality—their product becomes less and less relevant to business. As Joseph McGuire says, we now have nonbusiness business schools.[14] Increasingly, the product of the business school must be trained by business itself or else bypassed.

Administration, as Professor Lowi says, is rationality applied to social relations.[15] Administration involves rational choice; it is the result of decision making. It has outputs rather than outcomes. It takes place under prescriptions, the prescription of a plan of administration from higher authority (the "owner" or "his" representative) being influenced, it is hoped, by the universal prescriptions of rationality. The results as they affect individuals, therefore, are to be attributed to men (and to specific men, if we have enough insight into the process) rather than to natural laws or forces. Administration is an artificial system and is, therefore, always contentious.

Markets, societies, and other natural systems, on the other hand, have outcomes rather than outputs. These outcomes are statistical distributions and are, if they form repeatable patterns, natural laws—as opposed to the man-made laws of administration. Natural systems are self-regulating. The individual in this process appears to be a random factor relative to the decisions of any specifiable human being. The results of this process as they affect the individual, therefore, are not experienced as arbitrary and oppressive. They are fate. Or if they are not, then the individual "has no one to blame but himself." (To avoid this painful conclusion, it has long been customary to personify the natural system, and to "blame society," an essentially meaningless proposition, but one that is undoubtedly valuable psychologically.)

Responding to cues is less painful than responding to orders; it preserves the individual's sense of freedom and autonomy.[16] However, the use of cues instead of orders, or vice versa, tells us absolutely nothing about the amount of social control over the individual. Freedom cannot be contrasted to government or any other organization. Control in a natural system, which operates solely by cues, can be almost absolute, as the following old news story illustrates.

> Lucknow, India (*U.P.*)—Local doctors are hard pressed to save the life of a boy who apparently has lived in the jungle all his nine years. He is so terrified of humans he tries to bite the hands of those who feed him.
>
> The boy was picked up by police January 17. He was so emaciated he almost died, doctors said. And his health has not improved, because he has an intense dislike of cooked meat, milk, porridge, fruit juice and bread.
>
> "He only bursts into life when we produce some raw meat for him," one doctor said. His body is covered with scars, the doctor said, and his hands are like claws, with the nails long and talonlike and turned inward. [Note the difference between the natural-system criterion of "survival" and the criterion of "efficiency."]

A natural system is studied statistically, and the individual's behavior is subsumed under some probabalistic law; it is, in other words, determined—to the extent that anything is determined by probabilities. Artificial-system, prescriptive laws, on the other hand, the orders of a conscious, organizational, decision-making process, presume a free individual. If they did not, their issuance would be senseless. The individual is presumed to have the freedom to obey the law, which means, of course, that he also has the freedom to disobey it.

Organizations with their orders instead of cues, therefore, including the state and its laws, are in some way involved in the creation of freedom. The perception of more freedom within the statistical distributions of a natural system is more psychological (noncognitive) than real. The individual has a better chance under the rule of law, as Professor Lowi says, even if the law is not the best. He has a better chance under a regime of prescriptive rationality, a regime in which the many rationalities of the individuals and groups have been represented in some meaningful form and aggregated.

Notes

1. *The Problem Defined*

1. *Chicago Sun-Times*, Jan. 10, 1971.

2. James G. March and Herbert A. Simon, *Organizations* (New York: John Wiley & Sons, Inc., 1958), pp. 36 ff.

3. *Social Forces*, 17 (1940), pp. 560–68; also in Robert K. Merton *et al.*, eds., *Reader in Bureaucracy* (Glencoe, Ill.: The Free Press, 1952), pp. 361–71.

4. *Chicago Tribune*, June 24, 1931; and in Merton, *et al.*, eds., *Reader in Bureaucracy*, p. 366.

5. As it happened, Mr. Balchen eventually got his citizenship and had a successful career in the American Air Force. When he retired, he told the press that Admiral Byrd, the hero who first flew over the South Pole, had lied when he announced his flight over the pole. Thus, time puts a different perspective on all things.

6. On categorization as a characteristic quality of modern organization, and its relation to routinization, see Victor A. Thompson, *Modern Organization* (New York: Alfred A. Knopf, Inc., 1961), pp. 17–18.

7. Victor A. Thompson, "Bureaucracy in a Democratic Society," in Roscoe C. Martin, ed., *Public Administration and Democracy: Essays in Honor of Paul H. Appleby* (Syracuse, N. Y.: Syracuse University Press, 1965), pp. 205–26, at pp. 217–18. By permission of Syracuse University Press.

8. See Frank Marini, ed., *Toward a New Public Administration* (Scranton, Pa.: Chandler Publishing Company, 1971); and Marvin Surlsin and Alan Wolfe, eds., *An End to Political Science: The Caucus Papers* (New York: Basic Books, Inc., 1970); and Dwight Waldo, ed., *Public Administration in a Time of Turbulence* (Scranton, Pa.: Chandler Publishing Company, 1971).

9. Robert V. Presthus, *The Organizational Society* (New York: Alfred A. Knopf, Inc., 1962); and William H. Whyte, Jr., *The Organization Man* (Garden City, N. Y.: Doubleday Anchor Books, Doubleday & Co., Inc., 1957).

2. *The Nature of Modern Organizations*

1. See Victor A. Thompson, *Modern Organization*, and "Bureaucracy in a Democratic Society," in Roscoe Martin, ed., *Public Adminis-*

tration and Democracy: Essays in Honor of Paul Appleby, pp. 205–26; see also Emile Durkheim, *The Division of Labor in Society*, translated by George Simpson (New York: The Macmillan Co., 1933).

2. See Victor A. Thompson, *Modern Organization*, chapters 2 and 8.

3. Max Weber, *The Theory of Social and Economic Organization*, translated by A. M. Henderson and Talcott Parsons (New York: Oxford University Press, Inc., 1947); see also Daniel Lerner, "Toward a Communication Theory of Modernization," in Lucian W. Pye, ed., *Communications and Political Development* (Princeton, N.J.: Princeton University Press, 1963), pp. 327–30, and *The Passing of Traditional Society* (Glencoe, Ill.: The Free Press, 1958).

4. The analysis of organizations as both tools and natural systems, used throughout this book, is from Victor A. Thompson, *Organizations as Systems* (Morristown, N. J.: General Learning Press, 1973).

5. See F. William Howton, *Functionaries* (Chicago: Quadrangle Books, Inc., 1969); also Karl Mannheim, *Ideology and Utopia* (New York: Harcourt, Brace & Company, 1936), pp. 105–06. There is another role, always implied in decision-making situations. Instrumental decisions are based on "true" knowledge; other kinds are bets or neurotic. Therefore, a role of objective observer is always implied in tool or system construction. It will be discussed below.

6. The Florida state welfare agency, in self review, found about 8 percent illegal welfare recipients. (*Florida Times-Union*, Jan. 9, 1972.) In Illinois, the number of illegal welfare recipients goes up year by year and in July, 1974, was 12.9 percent of the total. (*Chicago Sun-Times*, July 18, 1974.) On December 20, 1973, HEW Secretary Weinberger said that "Taxpayers lose 15 cents of every dollar spent on welfare because more than 40 percent of all welfare families are either ineligible or incorrectly paid." (*Florida Times-Union*, Dec. 21, 1973.) A related phenomenon is the apparently increasing tendency for lower-level officials to try to dictate policy by mass confrontation with superiors or by committing illegal acts such as giving secret policy documents to a hostile newspaper or newspaperman. As James Reston said of the leaking of classified national-security documents to columnist Jack Anderson and his publication of them, the practice represents "defiant disclosures of the *true facts* by officials who have lost faith in the judgment and truthfulness of their superiors [my italics]." (*Florida Times-Union*, Jan. 9, 1972.) This unconscious disclosure of a vicious bias is classic. An Illinois state welfare official has openly accused case workers of making subjective judgments in determining the amount of a welfare payment. (*Chicago Sun-Times*, Aug. 9, 1973.)

7. Frank Marini, ed., op. cit.

8. I mildly apologize to the academic practitioners of the "new public administration" for such terms as "theft" and "subversion." They are to be understood in the context of the argument and as such are semimetaphorical.

9. This, I take it, is nevertheless the program of the new public administration. In Max Weber's view, modern, efficient, rational administration became possible only when this practice was largely eliminated.

10. The following discussion depends heavily on Fred Riggs, "Agraria and Industria—Toward a Typology of Comparative Administration," in William J. Siffin, ed., *Toward the Comparative Study of Administration* (Bloomington, Ind.: Indiana University Press, 1957), pp. 23–116; and his *Administration in Developing Countries* (Boston: Houghton Mifflin Company, 1964); and many other writings of the Comparative Administration Group, too numerous to mention.

11. For a good demonstration of the applicability of the Riggs model to a transitional society, see Martin Harry Greenberg, *Bureaucracy and Development: A Mexican Case Study* (Lexington, Mass.: D. C. Heath & Co., 1970). Among other characters, the "intermediary," or "five percenter," is well described.

12. See Herbert A. Simon, Donald W. Smithburg, and Victor A. Thompson, *Public Administration* (New York: Alfred A. Knopf, Inc., 1950), chapters 13 and 14; Victor A. Thompson, *The Regulatory Process in OPA Rationing* (New York: Kings Crown Press, 1950), *passim;* and Victor A. Thompson, *Bureaucracy and Innovation* (University, Ala.: University of Alabama Press, 1969), chapter 4.

13. Robert K. Merton "Bureaucratic Structure and Personality," *Social Forces,* 17 (1940), pp. 560–68. See also F. William Howton, *Functionaries,* pp. 36–41; Karl Mannheim, *Ideology and Utopia* (New York: Harcourt, Brace & Company, 1936), especially pp. 105–106; Reinhard Bendix, *Max Weber: An Intellectual Portrait* (Garden City, N. Y.: Doubleday & Company, 1960), pp. 455–56.

14. See Herbert A. Simon, *Administrative Behavior* (New York: The Macmillan Company, 1947); Herbert A. Simon and James G. March, *Organizations* (New York: John Wiley & Sons, Inc., 1958); and Victor A. Thompson, *Decision Theory, Pure and Applied* (New York: General Learning Press, 1971).

15. See many of the entries in Francis E. Rourke, *Bureaucratic Power in National Politics,* 2nd ed., (Boston: Little, Brown & Company, 1972); Alan A. Altshuler, *The Politics of the Federal Bureaucracy* (New York: Dodd, Mead & Company, 1968); the symposium on citizen involvement, *Public Administration Review,* vol. 32, no. 3 (May–June, 1972). See also Samuel P. Huntington, "Congressional

Responses to the Twentieth Century," and Richard E. Neustadt, "Politicians and Bureaucrats," both in David B. Truman, ed., *The Congress and America's Future* (Englewood Cliffs, N. J.: Prentice-Hall, Inc., Spectrum Books, 1965). Note, also, the widespread criticism of the FBI and the Corps of Engineers for making their own political decisions—i.e., for practicing "substantive rationality."

16. See, for example, Fred W. Riggs, *Administration in Developing Countries*; Francis E. Rourke, *Bureaucratic Power*, part VI; and Victor A. Thompson, *Organizations as Systems*.

17. See Dean S. Dorn and Gary L. Long, "Sociology and the Radical Right: A Critical Analysis," *The American Sociologist*, vol. 7, no. 5 (May, 1972). The authors conclude that the "political right may be viewed as a problem for United States democracy because right-wingers reject the liberal values of 'enlightened upper and upper middle-class social scientists'" (p. 8). See also F. William Howton, *Functionaries*, especially pp. 36–41.

18. See David Rogers, *110 Livingston Street* (New York: Random House, 1968). On the conditions for natural-system development, see George Homans, *The Human Group* (New York: Harcourt Brace & World, Inc., 1950).

19. These terms were developed by Talcott Parsons and are now used in virtually all cross-cultural studies. See his *The Social System* (Glencoe, Ill.: The Free Press, 1951), pp. 58–67; and Talcott Parsons and Edward A. Shils, eds., *Toward a General Theory of Action* (Cambridge, Mass.: Harvard University Press, 1959), p. 77.

20. As Max Weber said, the modern functionary carries out his duties *sine ira ac studio*, without passion or enthusiasm.

21. See Lucian W. Pye, *Aspects of Political Development* (Boston: Little, Brown & Company, 1969), and Samuel P. Huntington, *Political Order in Changing Societies* (New Haven, Conn.: Yale University Press, 1968).

22. Although this report is widely circulated, I have not been able to find the source for it. However, the use of the "nonperson" sanction by primitive peoples is well documented. See Lucien Levy-Bruhl, *Primitive Mentality*, translated by Lilian A. Clare (Boston: Beacon Press, 1966), p. 280; also see Theodore R. Sarbin, "Role Theory," in Gardner Lindzey, *Handbook of Social Psychology*, vol. I (Cambridge, Mass.: Addison-Wesley Publishing Co., Inc., 1954), p. 235.

23. In the kibbutz, small-group emotional conditioning and socialization comes largely from peers, but it is still there. This form of childhood training seems to produce a more apathetic adult. See Bruno

Bettelheim, *Children of the Dream* (New York: The Macmillan Company, 1969).

3. *Solutions: Personnel Administration*

1. Our foreign aid program has been beset by this difficulty for some time. Many Americans have expected gratitude and been puzzled by the amount of foreign jubilation over our reverses. See the remarks by Paul Hoffman, the Marshall Plan administrator, concerning the AID program, in *Time* magazine, Jan. 17, 1972. St. Vincent de Paul told his disciples to deport themselves so that the poor "will forgive you the bread you give them."

2. See Sam Schulman, "Basic Functional Roles in Nursing: Mother Surrogate and Healer," in E. Gartly Jaco, ed., *Patients, Physicians and Illness* (Glencoe, Ill.: The Free Press, 1958), pp. 528-37. The bureaucratization of the hospital is making it less and less possible for nurses to indulge this need to help others. Here, too, compassion is incompatible with professional efficiency and the specialization of function.

3. This kind of staffing (by attitude or program identification) created many problems for various programs of the Office of Economic Opportunity, such as the legal-services program. British administrators generally take a dim view of strong program commitments by civil servants. That is for the politicians. See, for example, H. E. Dale, *The Higher Civil Service of Great Britain* (London: Oxford University Press, 1941). He was formerly assistant secretary, Ministry of Agriculture and Fisheries. See also E. N. Gladden, *The Civil Service: Its Problems and Future* (London: Staples Press Ltd., 1945). He was in the Service for thirty years. See also Peter du Sautoy, *The Civil Service* (London: Oxford University Press, 1957).

4. *Solutions: Organization Development and Sensitivity Training*

1. See Warren Bennis, *Changing Organization* (New York: McGraw-Hill Book Co., 1966), and *Organization Development* (Reading, Mass.: Addison-Wesley Publishing Co., 1969); Paul R. Lawrence and Jay W. Lorsch, *Developing Organizations* (Reading, Mass.: Addison-Wesley Publishing Co., 1969); Rensis Lickert, *The Human Organization* (New York: McGraw-Hill Book Co., 1967); Chris Argyris, *Interpersonal Competence and Organizational Effectiveness* (Homewood, Ill.: Dorsey Press, 1962), and *Organization Development* (New Haven, Conn.: Yale University Press, 1960); Robert R. Blake and Jane Srygley Mouton, *Building a Dynamic Corporation Through Grid Organizational Development* (Reading, Mass.: Addison-Wesley Publishing Co., 1969);

Richard Beckhard, *Organization Development: Strategies and Models* (Reading, Mass.; Addison-Wesley Publishing Co., 1969); H. J. Leavitt, "Unhealthy Organizations," in H. J. Leavitt and L. Pondy, eds., *Reading in Managerial Psychology* (Chicago: The University of Chicago Press, 1964).

2. *Changing Organizations*, chapter 3, at p. 52. The quotation from Marie Jahoda is from *Current Concepts of Positive Mental Health* (New York: Basic Books, Inc., 1958).

3. See Victor A. Thompson, *Modern Organization*, pp. 183–86; and Edward A. Shils, "Primary Groups in the American Army," in Robert K. Merton and Paul F. Lazarsfeld, eds., *Continuities in Social Research: Studies in the Scope and Method of "The American Soldier"* (Glencoe, Ill.: The Free Press, 1950). The continuing differentiation and autonomy of subsystems is one of the most profound natural-system processes. It allows integration of individuals into the subsystem which would not be possible in the larger system as a whole. If I accept values A and B but reject C, D, and E, I cannot cooperate with the system ABCDE, but I could cooperate with system A and system B if they were differentiated out. In this way, boundary maintenance becomes decisive for the maintenance of cooperation.

4. See Arthur H. Brayfield and Walter H. Crockett, "Employee Attitudes and Employee Performance," *Psychological Bulletin,* 52 (1955), pp. 396–424; Edward E. Lawler, III and Lyman W. Porter, "The Effect of Performance on Job Satisfaction," *Industrial Relations, a Journal of Economy and Society,* 7 (October, 1967), pp. 20–28; Robert J. House and Lawrence A. Wigdor, "Herzberg's Dual-Factor Theory of Job Satisfaction and Motivation: A Review of the Evidence and a Criticism," *Personnel Psychology,* 20 (1967), pp. 369–89; and Charles L. Hulin and Milton R. Blood, "Job Enlargement, Individual Differences, and Worker Responses," *Psychological Bulletin,* 69 (1968), pp. 41–55.

5. Ralf Dahrendorf, in his book *Class and Class Conflict in Industrial Society* (Stanford: Stanford University Press, 1959), thinks in terms of concrete groups of people called "classes" rather than in terms of systems. To him, therefore, the inevitable conflict is between the group-superiors—and the group-subordinates. Superiors, however, are also under the control of the natural system to some extent. The conflict is between systems, the behavioral one (natural) and the prescriptive one (artificial), or between self-interest and duty.

6. It was developed by the National Training Laboratories of the National Education Association. For descriptions of the method see Leland Bradford, Jack R. Gibb, and Kenneth D. Benne, eds., *T-Group*

Theory and Laboratory Method (New York: John Wiley & Sons, Inc., 1964). For a short description, see Herbert A. Shepard, "The T-Group as Training in Observant Participation," in Warren G. Bennis, Kenneth D. Benne, and Robert Chin, eds., *The Planning of Change* (New York: Holt, Rinehart & Winston, 1962). A more recent book is Robert T. Golembiewski, *Renewing Organizations* (Itasca, Ill.: F. E. Peacock Pub., Inc., 1972).

7. For example, see Paul C. Buchanan (Associate Professor of Education at Yeshiva University), "Laboratory Training and Organization Development," *Administrative Science Quarterly*, 14 (September, 1969), pp. 466–77. He says, however, that evidence for organization change is not impressive. See also Herbert A. Shepard, "Changing Interpersonal and Intergroup Relationships in Organizations," chapter 26 in James G. March, ed., *Handbook of Organizations* (Chicago: Rand McNally & Company, 1965), pp. 1,115–143.

8. See especially John P. Campbell and Marvin D. Dunnette, "Effectiveness of T-Group Experiences in Managerial Training and Development," *Psychological Bulletin*, 70 (August, 1968). Also, see Robert J. House, "T-Group Education and Leadership Effectiveness: a Review of the Empirical Literature and a Critical Evaluation," *Personnel Psychology*, 20 (Spring, 1967); and G. S. Odiorne, "The Trouble with Sensitivity Training," *Training and Development Journal*, 17 (October, 1963). Warren Bennis says, "Sometimes the changes brought about simply 'fade out.' . . . In other cases, the changes have backfired and have had to be terminated . . . " (*Changing Organizations*, p. 174.) He says, further, "Relating change programs to harder criteria, such as productivity and economic and cost factors, was rarely attempted and was never, to my knowledge, successful." (Ibid., p. 172.) The most comprehensive evaluation is in Kurt Back, *Beyond Words* (New York: Russell Sage Foundation, 1972).

9. See the sources in the note above. In addition see A. J. M. Sykes, "The Effect of a Supervisory Training Course in Changing Supervisors' Perceptions and Expectations of the Role of Management," *Human Relations*, 15 (Summer, 1962), pp. 227–43.

10. See especially, George Homans, *The Human Group;* also see Dorwin Cartwright and Alvin Zander, eds., *Group Dynamics*, 3rd ed. (New York: Harper & Row, Publishers, 1968).

11. It is fair, though not necessary, to cite at this point David Riesman, Nathan Glazer, and Reuel Denney, *The Lonely Crowd* (Garden City, N. J.: Doubleday & Co., Inc., 1953).

12. Reported in Sylvia Porter's column, *Chicago Daily News,* May

23, 1960. Such practices are general throughout American business, according to *Modern Office Procedures*.

13. See Erving Goffman's discussion of these rituals in his paper, "On the Characteristics of Total Institutions," in his *Asylums* (Chicago: Aldine Publishing Co., 1961).

14. The following discussion of training is based on my paper *Organizations as Systems*.

15. See Edgar H. Schein, "Forces which Undermine Managerial Development," *California Managerial Review*, 5 (Summer, 1963), pp. 23–34; Kenneth R. Andrews, "Is Management Training Effective? 2. Measurement, Objectives, and Policy," *Harvard Business Review*, 35 (March/April, 1957), pp. 63–72; E. A. Fleishman, "Leadership Climate, Human Relations Training, and Supervisory Behavior," *Personnel Psychology*, 6 (1953), pp. 205–22; Center for Programs in Government Administration, "Education for Innovative Behavior in Executives," Cooperative Research Project No. 975 of the United States Office of Education, Department of Health, Education and Welfare; Harold Guetzkow, Garley A. Forehand and Bernard J. James, "An Evaluation of Educational Influence on Administrative Judgment," *Administrative Science Quarterly*, 6 (1961-62), pp. 483–500; and A. J. M. Sykes, "The Effect of a Supervisory Training Course in Changing Supervisors' Perceptions and Expectations of the Role of Management," op. cit. Sykes reports a case where 97 supervisors were given a human-relations course. Eighty-three later said it was a failure; 14 had no opinion; none said it was a success. Nineteen of them left the company within the year; 27 others applied for jobs elsewhere in the company. In the previous two years, only 2 supervisors had left the company. The supervisors said that the attitudes of senior management had not changed (they had also taken such a course at the same time). In other words, the expectations of the supervisors had changed, but the organization had not.

16. Amatai Etzioni, *A Comparative Analysis of Complex Organizations* (New York: The Free Press, 1961), pp. 119 ff. So rare are people who can play both expressive and instrumental leadership roles, that they have been called "great men." See E. F. Borgatta, R. F. Bales, and A. S. Couch, "Some Findings Relevant to the Great Man Theory of Leadership," *American Sociological Review*, 19 (1954), pp. 755–59.

5. *Solutions: Smaller Units*

1. *Time*, Jan. 3, 1972, attributes this statement to Yale physicist D. Allen Bromley. On distortions in the opposition to DDT, see various speeches and remarks by Norman E. Borlaug.

2. Reported by Frank Carey of Associated Press in the *Florida Times-Union*, Jan. 9, 1972.

3. See James R. Bright, *Automation and Management* (Cambridge, Mass.: Graduate School of Business Administration, Harvard University, 1958).

4. See Warren G. Bennis, *Changing Organizations,* chapter 1. Bennis believes work will increasingly be performed in temporary, interdisciplinary project groups, even though a larger coordinating framework may remain. See also William H. Reynolds, "The Executive Synecdoche," *Business Topics* (Autumn, 1969), pp. 21–29. Thomas L. Whisler takes much the same view and adds the idea that the replacement of men by machines, especially computors, makes for smaller organizations. See his *Executives and Their Jobs—the Changing Organizational Structure* (Chicago: Selected Papers No. 9, Graduate School of Business, The University of Chicago). Peter F. Drucker believes hierarchial structures are doomed because they veto and stifle innovation; see his *The Age of Discontinuity* (New York: Harper & Row, 1969). See also Alvin Toffler, *Future Shock* (New York: Random House, Inc., 1970), to the same effect.

5. Samuel P. Huntington, "Interservice Competition and the Roles of the Armed Services," *American Political Science Review,* 55 (March, 1961), pp. 40–52.

6. See William H. Reynolds, op. cit.

7. See Donald W. Collier, "An Innovation System for the Larger Company," *Research Management* (September, 1970), pp. 341–48; Theodore Levitt, *The Marketing Mode: Pathways to Corporate Growth* (New York: McGraw-Hill Book Co., Inc., 1970), especially chapter 7; Tom Burns and B. M. Stalker, *The Management of Innovation* (London: Tavistock Publications, 1959); Victor A. Thompson, *Bureaucracy and Innovation;* James D. Hlavacek and Victor A. Thompson, "Bureaucracy and New Product Innovation," *Academy of Management Journal,* 16 (September, 1972), pp. 361–72; Robert Townsend, *Up the Organization* (New York: Alfred A. Knopf, Inc., 1970); Hubert Kay, "Harnessing the R. and D. Monster," *Fortune* (January, 1965), beginning at p. 160; "How Bell Labs Answer Calls for Help," *Business Week* (January, 1971), pp. 38–44; Donald C. Pelz and Frank M. Andrews, *Scientists in Organizations: Productive Climates for Research and Development* (New York; John Wiley & Sons, Inc., 1966); and Louis Saltanoff, "The Innovation Myth," *Industrial Research* (August, 1971), pp. 45–46.

8. See S. C. Gilfillan, *The Sociology of Invention* (Federalsburg, Md.: Stowell, 1935); and Bureau of Economic Research, *The Rate and*

Direction of Inventive Activities (Princeton, N. J.: Princeton University Press, 1962), *passim;* Simon Marcson, *The Scientist in American Industry* (Princeton, N. J.: Industrial Relations School, 1960); and Richard R. Nelson, "The Economics of Invention: A Survey of the Literature," *Journal of Business,* 23 (April, 1959), pp. 114.

9. See Victor A. Thompson, *Decision Theory, Pure and Applied;* also *Bureaucracy and Innovation,* pp. 26–27.

10. See Jay W. Lorsch, *Product Innovation and Organization* (New York: The Macmillan Company, 1965).

11. During the 1960s, when racial pressure on the Chicago Board of Education became too strong, Superintendent of Schools Benjamin Willis suddenly, and without advance consultation, appointed an "Assistant Superintendent for Integration." See Victor A. Thompson, "The Innovative Organization," in Fred D. Carver and Thomas J. Sergiovanni, eds., *Organizations and Human Behavior: Focus on Schools* (New York: McGraw-Hill Book Co., 1969). "In order to give the discipline continued thrust and new programs in dealing with its minorities, the ASA has added Dr. Maurice Jackson to its staff as Executive Specialist for Race and Minority Relations." See *The American Sociologist,* vol. 7, no. 1 (January, 1972), p. 1. Note even the bureaucratic assignment of the most universal of activities in a National Science Foundation. See Don Price, *Government and Science* (New York: University Press, 1954). Innovation is segregated in "R and D units." See Thompson, *Bureaucracy and Innovation.* This widespread administrative practice is a manifestation of an even wider one— "solving" problems by labeling them. The first Hoover Commission recommended a Board of *Impartial* Analysis for Engineering and Architectural Projects "for making certain that only projects which are economically and socially justifiable are recommended for approval." See *Report on the Department of Interior,* p. 5. It is not only in the United States that we find word-magic administration. The Swedish Constitution of 1809, still in force, creates the office of *Justitiekansler,* who is to be "an able and impartial man." See Brian Chapman, *The Profession of Government* (London: Unwin University Books, 1959), p. 246. Problems are frequently "solved" by naming them in amended administrative regulations. The administrator can then disarm his critics by pointing to the regulations to prove that the matter is "covered," and strangely enough, this gesture usually stems the criticism. See Victor A. Thompson, *The Regulatory Process in OPA Rationing.*

12. See James D. Hlavacek, *An Empirical Analysis of Managing Product Innovation in Complex Chemical Organizations,* unpublished Ph.D. dissertation, College of Business Administration, University of

Illinois, Urbana, 1971; also James D. Hlavacek and Victor A. Thompson, "Bureaucracy and New Product Innovation," op. cit.; and *Venture Management,* a survey of venture management operations in 36 large American industrial companies by Towers, Perrin, Forster and Crosby, Consultants, in 1970.

13. See Morris I. Stein and Shirley J. Vidich, eds., *Creativity and the Individual* (Glencoe, Ill.: The Free Press, 1960), and, by the same authors, *Survey of Psychological Literature in the Area of Creativity With View Toward Needed Research* (New York: Research Center for Human Relations and New York University Press, 1962).

14. Alvin Gouldner reported this kind of behavior in his study of "Red tape as a Social Problem," in Robert K. Merton, *et al.,* eds., *Reader in Bureaucracy* (Glencoe, Ill.: The Free Press, 1952), pp. 410–18.

15. Martin Landau, "Redundancy, Rationality, and the Problem of Duplication and Overlap," in *Public Administration Review,* 29 (July-August, 1969), pp. 346–58.

16. Although most government services are either not amenable to competition or result from its breakdown, William Niskanen, Jr., suggests that we adopt the principle of competition as a means of bringing the bureaucracy under control. See his *Bureaucracy and Representative Government* (Chicago: Aldine-Atherton Publishing Co., 1971). There were economists at the Rand Corporation who developed the idea of rationalizing government expenditures by "cost/benefit" analysis, in dollars, into a "new" form of government budgeting and decision making called Planning, Programming, Budgeting (PPB). See David Novick, *Program Budgeting,* a Rand Corporation Study (Washington, D. C.: Government Printing Office, 1965); and also Fremont J. Lyden and Ernest G. Miller, eds., *Planning Programming Budgeting: A Systems Approach to Management* (Chicago: Markham Publishing Co., 1967). The classic statement of how government originates in failures of the economic system is Robert A. Dahl and Charles E. Lindblom, *Politics, Economics and Welfare* (New York: Harper & Bros., 1953).

17. See Herbert A. Simon, Donald W. Smithburg and Victor A. Thompson, *Public Administration,* chapter 21.

18. *Gainesville Sun.,* Sept. 7, 1973.

19. *Gainesville Sun.,* Oct. 29, 1972, from a *New York Times* release.

20. See the discussion on "feedback" in Raymond A. Bauer, ed., *Social Indicators* (Cambridge, Mass.: MIT Press, 1966), chapter 5.

21. Fred Riggs has made this point very strongly in "Agraria and Industria—Toward a Typology of Comparative Administration," op. cit.

22. See Erving Goffman, *Asylums.*

6. *Solutions: Combining Roles*

1. Philip Selznick, *Leadership in Administration* (Evanston, Ill.: Row, Peterson & Co., 1957).
2. See Bert L. Metzger and Jerome A. Colletti, *Does Profit Sharing Pay?* (Evanston, Ill.: Profit Sharing Research Foundation, 1971).
3. On the psychological resolution of role conflict in organizations, see Robert L. Kahn, *et al., Organizational Stress* (New York: John Wiley & Sons, Inc., 1964).

7. *Solutions: Political Machines and Prefectural Administration*

1. Talcott Parsons, Robert F. Bales, and Edward A. Shils, *Working Papers in the Theory of Action* (Glencoe, Ill.: The Free Press, 1953); Robert F. Bales, "Task Roles and Social Roles in Decision-making Groups," in Leonard D. White, ed., *The State of the Social Sciences* (Chicago: The University of Chicago Press, 1956), pp. 148–61; and Amatai Etzioni, *The Comparative Analysis of Complex Organizations,* pp. 91 ff.
2. See Lucian W. Pye, *Aspects of Political Development;* Samuel P. Huntington, *Political Order in Changing Societies;* Fred Riggs, *Administration in Developing Countries*; Martin Harry Greenburg, *Bureaucracy and Development: A Mexican Case Study.*
3. For a good short discussion see Fred I. Greenstein, *The American Party System and the American People* (Englewood Cliffs, N. J.: Prentice-Hall, Inc., 1964).
4. See Brian Chapman, *The Prefects and Provincial France* (London: Allen & Unwin, 1955); Gabriel A. Almond and James S. Coleman, eds., *The Politics of the Developing Areas* (Princeton, N. J.: Princeton University Press, 1960), "Introduction"; Gabriel A. Almond and G. Bingham Powell, Jr., *Comparative Politics* (Boston: Little, Brown & Company, 1966), chapter 3; Samuel P. Huntington, *Political Order in Changing Societies,* p. 29; and James W. Fesler, "The Political Role of Field Administration," in Ferrel Heady and Sybil L. Stokes, *Papers in Comparative Public Administration* (Ann Arbor, Mich.: Institute of Public Administration, The University of Michigan, 1962), pp. 117–43.
5. On France, see Roy C. Macridis in Samuel E. Finer, Roy C. Macridis, Karl W. Deutsch, and Vernon Aspaturian, *Modern Political Systems: Europe* (Englewood Cliffs, N. J.: Prentice-Hall, Inc., 1968), p. 203. For Italy, see Giovanni Sartori, "European Political Parties:

110 Notes to Chapter Seven

The Case of Polarized Pluralism," in Joseph LaPalombara and Myron Weiner, eds., *Political Parties and Political Development* (Princeton, N. J.: Princeton University Press, 1966), pp. 140ff. (This book also discusses the French situation.)

6. See Brian Champan, op. cit.; James W. Fesler, op. cit.; and Goran Hyden, *Political Development in Rural Tanzania* (Nairobi, Kenya: East African Publishing House, 1969).

7. Much of the following discussion is based on Fred W. Riggs, "Agraria and Industria—Toward a Typology of Comparative Administration," op. cit., pp. 23–116, and his *Administration in Developing Countries.* See also Karl A. Wittfogel, *Oriental Despotism* (New Haven, Conn.: Yale University Press, 1957); Fred W. Riggs, *Thailand: The Modernization of a Bureaucratic Polity* (Honolulu: East-West Center Press, 1966). Also helpful are some of the papers in Joseph LaPalombara, ed., *Bureaucracy and Political Development* (Princeton, N. J.: Princeton University Press, 1963).

8. See especially previous citations to Fred W. Riggs, and in addition, his paper, "The Sala Model: An Ecological Approach to the Study of Comparative Administration," in Nimrod Raphaeli, ed., *Readings in Comparative Administration* (Boston: Allyn & Bacon, Inc., 1967). See also Victor A. Thompson, "Bureaucracy in a Democratic Society," in Roscoe C. Martin, *Public Administration and Democracy: Essays in Honor of Paul H. Appleby,* pp. 205–26.

9. See the papers in Ralph Braibanti, ed., *Asian Bureaucratic Systems Emergent from the British Imperial Tradition* (Durham, N. C.: Duke University Press, 1966). The term is used by James F. Guyot, "Bureaucratic Transformation in Burma," ibid., pp. 343–54. For other descriptions of the "frame," see Victor C. Ferkiss, "The Role of the Public Services in Nigeria and Ghana," in Ferrel Heady and Sybil L. Stokes, *Papers in Comparative Administration,* pp. 173–206; and J. Donald Kingsley, "Bureaucracy and Political Development, with Particular Reference to Nigeria," in Joseph LaPalombara, ed., *Bureaucracy and Political Development,* pp. 301–17.

10. For a generalized discussion of this phenomenon, see Victor A. Thompson, *Modern Organization,* as well as the sources cited immediately above.

11. See James W. Fesler, op. cit., and Brian Chapman, op. cit.

12. See papers in Ralph Braibanti, ed., op. cit.; also J. Donald Kingsley, op. cit.; and Goran Hyden, op. cit.

13. See Fred W. Riggs, *Administration in Developing Countries;* Lucian W. Pye, *Aspects of Political Development;* and Samuel P. Huntington, *Political Order in Changing Societies.*

14. See Victor A. Thompson, *Modern Organization,* and William R. Reynolds, "The Executive Synecdoche," op. cit.

15. The following discussion of prefectural field administration relies heavily on James W. Fesler, op. cit.; Brian Chapman, op. cit.; Jean Blondel, "Local Government and the Local Offices of Ministries in a French Department," *Public Administration,* 37 (Spring, 1959); and Robert C. Fried, *The Italian Prefects: A Study in Administrative Politics* (New Haven, Conn.: Yale University Press, 1963).

16. See Gladys M. Kammerer and John M. DeGrove, *Florida City Managers.* Studies in Public Administration No. 22, (Gainesville, Fla.: Public Administration Clearing Service, University of Florida, 1961).

17. See David S. Brown, "Strategies and Tactics of Public Administration Technical Assistance: 1945–1963," in John D. Montgomery and William J. Siffin, *Approaches to Development: Politics, Administration and Change* (New York: McGraw-Hill Book Co., 1966), pp. 185–223; also David Wurfel, "Foreign Aid and Social Reform in Political Development: A Philippine Case Study," *American Political Science Review,* 53 (June, 1959), pp. 456–82.

18. Herbert Kaufman, "Administrative Decentralization and Political Power," in Francis Rourke, *Bureaucratic Power in National Politics,* 2nd ed. (Boston: Little, Brown & Company, 1972), p. 390.

19. Gideon Sjoberg, Richard A. Bryner, and Buford Farris, "Bureaucracy and the Lower Class," *Sociology and Social Research,* 50 (April, 1966), pp. 325–37, and Frances Fox Piven, "Militant Civil Servants in New York City,'" *Transaction,* 7 (November, 1969), pp. 24–26, 55. The burden of the Sjoberg, *et al.,* article is that bureaucracy now reflects the dominant majority culture but should reflect the minority culture of the poor—those who have failed within the dominant culture. This startling proposal seems to have been a perennial theme with many sociologists and has recently been adopted by the "new left" for both public administration and political science.

20. Congress will not even allow the Budget Bureau to have field offices. See U. S. Senate, 90th Congress, 1st Session, Subcommittee of the Committee on Appropriations, *Hearings on H. R. 7501: Treasury, Post Office and Executive Office Appropriations for Fiscal Year 1968* (Washington, D. C.: Government Printing Office, 1967), pp. 973–90. Note also how the New York City Council and the Board of Estimates rebuffed Mayor John Lindsay's attempt to set up a number of "little city halls."

21. Kaufman, op. cit., p. 395.

22. See the discussion of the newest such device—the Federal Regional Councils—by Melvin B. Mogulof, "Federal Interagency

Action and Inaction: The Federal Regional Council Experience," *Public Administration Review,* vol. 32, no. 3 (May-June, 1972), pp. 232–40.
23. See Kaufman, op. cit.,; also Joseph F. Zimmerman, "Neighborhoods and Citizen Involvement," *Public Administration Review,* vol. 32, no. 3 (May-June, 1972), pp. 201–10; and James A. Riedel, "Citizen Participation: Myths and Realities," *Public Administration Review,* vol. 32, no. 3 (May-June, 1972), pp. 211–20. The difficulties of implementing the areal concept in this form of political decentralization to the level of impoverished neighborhoods are well described by Gary English, "The Trouble with Community Action," *Public Administration Review,* vol. 32, no. 3 (May-June, 1972), pp. 224–31. English is sympathetic to the idea.
24. See Kaufman's excellent summary of these difficulties, op. cit.
25. The best explanation for this decline comes from Samuel P. Huntington, *Political Order in Changing Societies.* Huntington argues that development brings new groups into the political arena. If political institutions are sufficiently developed to accomodate these new political actors, to articulate and aggregate their demands in a fashion satisfactory to them, change may take place within stability. Otherwise the political system becomes unstable, violence increases, rapid changes of political leadership take place by election, coup d'état, or even revolution. For the same idea, see Lucian W. Pye, *Aspects of Political Development.*

8. *Solutions: Assign to an Office—the Ombudsman*

1. Warren Dunham, "Community Psychiatry: the Newest Therapeutic Bandwagon," *Archives of General Psychiatry,* 12 (March, 1965), pp. 303–13. For what it is worth, Ralph Nader's organization has called "the Community Mental Health Center program a dismal failure. . . . Far from reducing the number of patients in state mental hospitals by treating them in a community setting near their home . . . six years of operation of the mental health program has actually seen a 4 percent rise in the in-patient population and a 50 percent rise in expenditures for state institutions." (William Hines, in the *Chicago Sun-Times,* July 23, 1972.)
2. Reported in Jack Anderson's column, the *Florida Times-Union,* Dec. 1, 1971.
3. The following discussion of the ombudsman rests upon Brian Chapman, *The Profession of Government* (London: Unwin University Books, 1959); Stanley V. Anderson, *Ombudsmen for American Government?* (Englewood Cliffs, N. J.: Prentice-Hall, Inc., 1968); Walter Gellhorn, *When Americans Complain* (Cambridge, Mass.: Harvard

University Press, 1966); L. Harold Levinson, ed., *Our Kind of Ombudsman*, Studies in Public Administration No. 32 (Gainesville, Fla.: Public Administration Clearing Service, 1970); Richard J. Carlson, ed., *University of Illinois Assembly on the Ombudsman* (Urbana, Ill.: The Institute of Government and Public Affairs, 1969); and Theodore J. Lowi, *The End of Liberalism* (New York: W. W. Norton & Company, Inc., 1969).

4. Andrew Shonfield, *Modern Capitalism* (London: Oxford University Press, 1965), p. 425.

5. See Anthony Downs, *Inside Bureaucracy* (Boston: Little, Brown & Company, 1967), and Theodore J. Lowi, op. cit.

6. Chapman, op. cit., pp. 251–52, and p. 259.

7. In one sense, administrative law develops because of this fact. See the Report of The Attorney General's Committee on Administrative Procedure, *Administrative Procedure in Government Agencies*, Senate Document No. 8, 77th Congress.

8. See Robert Gerwig and Wilson Freeman, "The Art of Military Ombudsmanship," in L. Harold Levinson, ed., *Our Kind of Ombudsman*, pp. 32-41.

9. Samuel Stouffer, *et al.*, *The American Soldier*, Volume I (Princeton, N. J.: Princeton University Press, 1949), pp. 398–401.

10. Chapman, op. cit., p. 427.

11. See any realistic description of bureaucratic behavior, for example, Aaron Wildavsky, *The Politics of The Budgetary Process* (Boston: Little, Brown & Company, 1964).

9. *Solutions: The "New Public Administration"*

1. See Frank Marini, ed., *Toward a New Public Administration: The Minnowbrook Perspective*. The *Public Administration Review* for January-February, 1974, was devoted almost entirely to this project.

2. Especially important is Alfred Shutz, *The Phenomenology of the Social World*, trans. by George Walsh and Frederick Lehnert (Evanston, Ill.: Northwestern University Press, 1967), because this book is specifically a criticism of the sociology of Max Weber.

3. See "Comment: Empirical Theory and the New Public Administration," in Marini, op. cit., p. 233. A similar, barely veiled threat can be found in Marvin Surkin and Alan Wolfe, eds., *An End to Political Science: The Caucus Papers*, chapter 3.

4. Erving Goffman, "On the Characteristics of Total Institutions," in his *Asylums*, pp. 1–124.

5. An interesting example of how the "less fortunate" person may feel was provided during a recent telethon to raise money for the Muscular

Dystrophy Association of America. During the telethon, "demonstrators afflicted with the disease paraded outside the broadcast and chanted, 'You're exploiting us!' . . . Spokesmen for the demonstrators accused the Association of failing to let the disabled sit on policy boards, failing to hire the disabled and exploiting them in advertising." (From an Associated Press report in the *Chicago Sun-Times*, Sept. 5, 1972.)

6. Theodore J. Lowi, *The End of Liberalism*.

7. See Michael J. Oakeshott, *Rationalism in Politics and Other Essays* (New York: Basic Books Publishing Co., 1962), pp. 1–36. He champions experience over codified knowledge, "technique," or "doctrine."

8. Victor A. Thompson, *The Regulatory Process in OPA Rationing*, pp. 196–203.

9. Taken from a report in the *Champaign-Urbana News-Gazette*, Mar. 29, 1969.

10. In 1968, "the court ordered CHA to build three units in white areas for every one in black areas, and indicated that no units would be built in black or 'mixed' areas until 700 were built in white areas." " . . . CHA provided only 600 units of family public housing in 1970–72 . . . ; and in 1973 it announced 50 units . . . " (J.S. Fuerst, "Death Wish for Public Housing," *Chicago Sun-Times*, June 24, 1973.) "Public housing in Chicago is in a state of near paralysis." (Ibid.)

11. The following discussion of public-problem solving depends heavily upon David Braybrooke and Charles E. Lindblom, *A Strategy of Decision* (New York: The Free Press of Glencoe, 1963), and Charles E. Lindblom, *The Policy-Making Process* (Englewood Cliffs, N. J.: Prentice-Hall, Inc., 1968).

12. See, for example, Harold J. Spaeth, *An Introduction to Supreme Court Decision Making* (San Francisco: Chandler Publishing Company, 1965).

13. Morton Kondrache in the *Chicago Sun-Times*, Aug. 31, 1972. For a brief historical statement of the development of the institution of political representation, see Francis G. Wilson, *The Elements of Modern Politics* (New York: McGraw-Hill Book Company, Inc., 1936), chapter 14.

14. Talcott Parsons and Edward A. Shils, eds., *Toward a General Theory of Action*, p. 77. The other choices are between affectivity and affective neutrality; particularism and universalism; ascription and achievement; and diffuseness and specificity. Apparently Parsons has had second thoughts with regard to the self *vs.* collectivity choice and feels it "must be matched by a second one which . . . I have called the 'instrumental-consummatory' distinction." See Talcott Parsons, "The

Point of View of the Author," in Max Black, ed., *Social Theories of Talcott Parsons* (Englewood Cliffs, N. J.: Prentice-Hall, Inc., 1961), p. 330; also "Pattern Variables Revisited," *American Sociological Review*, 25 (August, 1960), pp. 467–83.

15. *Chicago Sun-Times*, Aug. 5, 1972.

16. Ibid., Aug. 6, 1972.

17. *Gainesville Sun*, Feb. 9, 1974.

18. *Chicago Sun-Times*, Aug. 6, 1972.

19. Ibid., Aug. 26, 1973.

20. Mark Finston in the *Florida Times-Union*, Mar. 3, 1972.

21. Donald W. Thomas and Jean Mayer, "The Search for the Secret of Fat," *Psychology Today*, 7 (September, 1973), p. 74. Fat women have one-third the chance of getting into the college of their choice as nonfat women.

22. B. B. Schaffer, "The Concept of Preparation: Some Questions about the Emergence of New States and the Transfer of Systems of Government," mimeographed, University of Queensland.

23. *Champaign-Urbana News-Gazette*, Mar. 4, 1971. See the literature on reference-group theory, for example, Robert K. Merton, *Social Theory and Social Structure* (Glencoe, Ill.: The Free Press, 1957), chapters 8 and 9; see also David Braybrooke and Charles E. Lindblom, *A Strategy of Decision*, chapter 8. "In a suit filed in U.S. District Court, David Dominguez, 26, charged that the Rockford (Illinois) Fire and Police Board of Commissioners discriminates against Mexican Americans as a class of citizens because of their shorter-than-average height." (*Chicago Sun-Times*, Aug. 31, 1972.) Pandora's Box is open.

24. *Florida Times-Union*, Feb. 9, 1974.

25. Reported in the *Chicago Sun-Times*, Aug. 17, 1972.

26. Peter I. Rose in a book review in *Contemporary Sociology*, 2 (January, 1973), p. 14.

27. *Florida Times-Union*, June 12, 1972.

28. *Gainesville Sun*, Feb. 9, 1974.

29. See Michael Novak, *The Rise of the Unmeltable Ethnics* (New York: The Macmillan Company, 1971).

30. From a United Press International report. In a recent issue of *Commentary*, Milton Himmelfarb muses whimsically: "I envy the young and the young in heart, who do not experience my occasional difficulties in grasping that while American women, who are more than 50 percent, are a minority, American Jews, who are fewer than 3 percent, are not a minority." See "McGovern and the Jews: A Debate," with Nathan Glazer, *Commentary*, 54 (September, 1972), pp. 43–51, at p. 49.

31. *Chicago Sun-Times,* Aug. 8, 1972.

32. Martin Patchen in a letter to *The American Sociologist,* 7 (May, 1972), pp. 15–16.

33. Ibid.

34. Barbara R. Lorch, "Reverse Discrimination in Hiring in Sociology Departments: A Preliminary Report," *The American Sociologist,* 8 (August, 1973), pp. 116–20. The mythical nature of the charges of sex discrimination in Sociology departments is carefully demonstrated by Julie C. Wolfe, Melvin L. DeFleur, and Walter L. Slocum in "Sex Discrimination in Hiring Practices of Graduate Sociology Departments: Myths and Realities," *The American Sociologist,* 8 (November, 1973), pp. 159–65. The bitter and emotional response of the ASA Committee on the Status of Women in Sociology was sad for reason but understandable as equity politics. Ibid., pp. 165–67.

35. Personal communication from an academic vice-president in a Chicago university.

36. *Chicago Sun-Times,* Aug. 26, 1973.

37. Ibid., Aug. 12, 1972.

38. Perhaps I should not be pessimistic. The more experienced elements of the Democratic Party reasserted themselves very quickly after the 1972 debacle.

39. On the very substantial institutional implications that may attach to simple age differences, see the reports on age sets in some primitive tribes, for example, H. E. Lambert, *Kikuyu Social and Political Institutions* (London: Oxford University Press, 1956).

40. Why, for example, has a Men's Liberation Movement not yet appeared? The World Health Organization reports that the average life expectancy of American men is 66.6 years while that of American women is 74.1. Men's life expectancy is declining; women's is going up. Surely 7.5 years of life more for women is one of the greatest discriminations that can be imagined. Furthermore, women, partly because they live longer, own two-thirds of the wealth of this country. (The WHO report was cited in the *Chicago Sun-Times,* Aug. 9, 1972.) There are 72.2 percent as many men as women over 65; by 1990 this percentage will be 67.5, according to the U. S. census bureau.

41. For example, in a commencement address to the New York Medical College: "for every man, woman and child in the United States we spent in 1969: $410 on national defense, $125 on the war in Vietnam, $19 on the space program, $19 in foreign aid, and only 89 cents on cancer research." Of course, we spent less on thousands of other things than we spent on cancer research. There are few greater or more common misuses of figures than this.

42. Note, for example, the following treatment of student revolts by a young sociology professor: "This is precisely what happens in almost every student revolt, for the students correctly perceive that many decisions are against their best interests, that they are systematically excluded from legitimate channels, and that they can influence decisions if they work together. Excluded from participating in the formal system, they turn to nonformal forms of partisan influence." J. Victor Baldridge, *Power and Conflict in the University* (New York: John Wiley & Sons, Inc., 1971), p. 140. This explanation is rationalist, absolutist, and biased. Any possibility of student pathology is excluded. He leaves out the "just-for-the-hell-of-it" theory, the boredom theory, the conspiracy theory, the permissive-child-rearing theory, the affluence theory, the spoiled-brat theory, the *Weltschmerz* theory, the youth-revolt theory, the failure-of-socialization-into-subordinate-roles theory, etc. He does not explain why the phenomenon appeared when it did in the 1960s, why it appeared everywhere at once, and why it now appears to have stopped. His explanation is ideological.

43. Erich Goode, book review in *Contemporary Sociology: A Journal of Reviews,* vol. 1, no. 3 (May, 1972), pp. 207–09, at p. 209. On schizophrenia and labeling, see R. D. Laing, *The Politics of the Family and Other Essays* (New York: Pantheon Books, 1971). For more on labeling theory, see also H. S. Becker, "Whose Side Are We On?," *Social Problems,* 14 (Winter), pp. 239–47; K. T. Erickson, "Notes on the Sociology of Deviance," in H. S. Becker, ed., *The Other Side* (New York: The Free Press, 1964); and E. M. Lemert, *Human Deviance, Social Problems and Social Control* (Englewood Cliffs, N. J.: Prentice-Hall, Inc., 1967).

44. See footnote 38.

45. Reported in the *Champaign-Urbana News-Gazette,* June 21, 1971.

46. Reported in the *Chicago Sun-Times,* Sept. 9, 1970.

47. *Chicago Sun-Times,* July 23, 1974.

48. For the development in this country of "poor people," as opposed to "poor stages" in a life span, see Daniel P. Moynihan, "Income by Right," in three parts, *The New Yorker,* Jan. 13, 20, and 27, 1973. "According to a recent University of Michigan study, 45 percent of all Americans were eligible for welfare payments at one time or another over a recent six-year period." (*Chicago Sun-Times,* July 18, 1974.) Most people are among "the poor" at some time during their lives.

49. See Ayn Rand's horrifying account of the early days of the Russian Revolution in *We The Living* (New York: The New American Library, Inc., 1959). This book was originally published by Random

House in 1936. Miss Rand knows what she is talking about. Born in Russia, she lived through this period.

50. See F. William Howton, *Functionaries,* pp. 54–61, and Dean S. Dorn and Gary L. Long, "Sociology and the Radical Right: A Critical Analysis," op. cit.

10. *Solutions: Changing Personalities, Changing Organizations*

1. Two examples will illustrate the general point discussed in this section. In East Africa, most people have limited monetary needs, most of their needs being satisfied in the traditional areas of their lineages. They are not, hence, committed to the labor market and have a very high turnover rate. Skilled labor, however, has a substantial investment of time and ego in skills and tends to be committed to the labor market. Therefore, industries that depend upon semiskilled labor, where there is a high investment in training and high labor turnover, are not competitive. Industries that depend upon either unskilled or highly skilled labor may succeed. See Walter Elkan and Lloyd A. Fallers, "The Mobility of Labor," in Wilbert E. Moore and Arnold S. Feldman, *Labor Commitment and Social Change in Developing Areas* (New York: Social Science Research Council, 1960).

Many managements in this country try to encourage a company-wide identification and loyalty stronger than that to the small, intimate, "primary" work group as a means of increasing control in general and productivity in particular. But what kind of socialization processes would be needed to create this stronger indentification to the abstract, "secondary" grouping—the organization? Surely, so long as people are socialized in small primary groups—families—they will usually give their first loyalty to the smaller work group. Perhaps if all workers were socialized in secondary groups—say, orphanages—this management goal could be achieved.

2. See Daniel Lerner, *The Passing of Traditional Society;* also Daniel Lerner, "Toward a Communication Theory of Modernization," in Lucian W. Pye, ed., *Communications and Political Development,* pp. 327–50. See also Clark Kerr, John T. Dunlop, Frederick Harbison, and Charles A. Myers, *Industrialism and Industrial Man* (New York: Oxford University Press, 1964). Welfare and unemployment in industrial countries is also partly a problem of "modernization" so defined— the modernization of "personalities," interpreting that phrase broadly to mean the development of skills and attitudes consistent with the achievement of modern personal goals.

3. "Social Structure and Organization," in James March, ed., *Handbook of Organizations,* p. 153. For an empirical study and extended

analysis of the relations between family socialization, personality, and the kinds of organizations found in a society, see Daniel R. Miller and Guy E. Swanson, *The Changing American Parent* (New York: John Wiley & Sons, Inc., 1958). They found modern American family socialization (child-rearing practices) consistent with the needs of a bureaucratic rather than an entrepreneurial society.

The relation between socialization, personality and the structural-role needs of the society is heavily documented. For example, see Kurt Geiger, "Changing Political Attitudes in Totalitarian Society: A Case Study of the Role of the Family," *World Politics*, 8 (January, 1956), pp. 187–205; H. H. Golden, "Literacy and Social Change in Underdeveloped Countries," *Rural Society*, 20 (1955), pp. 1–7; John Gulick, "Conservatism and Change in a Lebanese Village," *Middle East Journal*, 8 (Summer, 1954), pp. 295–307; Raphael Patai, "The Dynamics of Westernization in the Middle East," *Middle East Journal*, 9 (Winter, 1955), pp. 1–16; and Melvin M. Tumin, "Some Dysfunctions of Institutional Imbalances," *Behavioral Science*, 1 (July, 1956), pp. 218–23.

4. See Fred W. Riggs, "The Sala Model: An Ecological Approach to the Study of Comparative Administration," in Nimrod Raphaeli, ed., *Readings in Comparative Administration*, pp. 412–32. See also Emile Durkheim, *Suicide*, trans. by John A. Spauline and George Simpson (Glencoe, Ill.: The Free Press, 1951).

5. A few years ago, for example, the Indian Institute of Public Opinion found that 65 percent of Indian farmers believed that you had to have influence ("pull") to get government help. The payment to officials of what Westerners would call "bribes" (*baksheesh*) to get the most elementary rights and services is very common in the underdeveloped countries. See Fred W. Riggs, op. cit. The practice has about the same moral status as tipping in modern countries.

6. For example, Sidney Hook, no right-winger, recently published a piece in *Encounter* magazine, not the voice of reaction, arguing that our system of criminal justice has become unbalanced, being oversolicitous of criminals and undersolicitous of victims. "The Rights of the Victims," *Encounter*, 38 (April, 1972), pp. 11–15. According to Gallup polls, most Americans agree.

7. See, for example, Ronald Inglehart, "The Silent Revolution in Europe: Inter-generational Change in Post-Industrial Society," *American Political Science Review*, 65 (December, 1971), pp. 991–1017; and John B. Miner, "Changes in Student Attitudes toward Bureaucratic Role Prescriptions during the 1960s," *Administrative Science Quarterly*, 16 (September, 1971), pp. 351–64. Also see A. H. Maslow, *Motiva-

tion and Personality (New York: Harper & Brothers, Publishers, 1954), especially chapter 5.

8. This argument is developed in Victor A. Thompson, *Bureaucracy and Innovation,* chapter 5.

9. Chester I. Barnard, *The Functions of the Executive* (Cambridge, Mass.: The Harvard University Press, 1938). See also Donald G. Malcolm and Alan J. Rowe, eds., *Management Control Systems* (New York: John Wiley & Sons, Inc., 1960), *passim.* See also Exodus 18:13–21, where Moses is advised by his father-in-law, Jethro, to set up a departmental system based on a span of control of ten to ease the problems of communications.

10. The potentialities are quite thoroughly discussed in Allen F. Weston, *Privacy and Freedom* (New York: Atheneum Publishers, 1967), chapter 7. See also Donald G. Malcolm and Alan J. Rowe, op. cit.

11. The metaphor is suggested by Erving Goffman, *The Presentation of Self in Everyday Life* (Garden City, N. Y.: Doubleday & Company, Inc., 1959), especially chapter 3.

12. For a discussion of PPB see Fremont J. Lyden and Ernest G. Miller, eds., *Planning Programming Budgeting: A Systems Approach to Management;* also *Public Administration Review,* vol. 26 (December, 1966), and vol. 29 (March-April, 1969). These issues are devoted in their entirety to PPB.

13. Allen Schick, *Budget Innovation in the States* (Washington, D. C.: The Brookings Institution, 1971); and "A Death in the Bureaucracy: The Demise of PPB," *Public Administrative Review,* 33 (March-April, 1973), pp. 146–56. The tacitly accepted model of the innovation process projects the heroic, unselfish innovator fighting the selfish, narrow-minded beneficiaries of the status quo. An equally plausible and useful model would project the selfish or neurotic advocate of change for change's sake being successfully resisted by analytical, heroic, unselfish critics of senseless or even damaging changes. PPB has been quietly abandoned by the federal government. See OMB Circular No. A-11, June 21, 1971.

14. Joseph W. McGuire, "The Collegiate Business School Today," *Collegiate News and Views,* 25 (Spring, 1972), pp. 1–5. A recent survey of 450 corporations showed that 77 percent found college graduates inadequately prepared. (*Florida Times-Union,* June 10, 1973.)

15. *The End of Liberalism,* pp. 30ff.

16. See especially Robert A. Dahl and Charles E. Lindblom, *Politics, Economics, and Welfare,* and many of the subsequent writings of

1965). See also B. F. Skinner, *Beyond Freedom and Dignity* (New York: Alfred A. Knopf, Inc., 1971).
Lindblom, for example, *The Intelligence of Democracy: Decision Making Through Mutual Adjustment* (New York: The Free Press,

Bibliography

Almond, Gabriel A., and G. Bingham Powell, Jr. *Comparative Politics.* Boston: Little, Brown & Company, 1966.

Almond, Gabriel A., and James S. Coleman, eds. *The Politics of Developing Areas.* Princeton, N. J.: The Princeton University Press, 1960.

Altshuler, Alan A., ed. *The Politics of the Federal Bureaucracy.* New York: Dodd, Mead & Company, 1968.

Anderson, Stanley V. *Ombudsmen for American Government.* Englewood Cliffs, N. J.: Prentice-Hall, 1968.

Andrews, Kenneth R. "Is Management Training Effective? 2. Measurement, Objectives, and Policy." *Harvard Business Review*, vol. 35 (March-April, 1957), pp. 63–72.

Argyris, Chris. *Organization Development.* New Haven, Conn.: Yale University Press, 1960.

Argyris, Chris. *Interpersonal Competence and Organizational Effectiveness.* Homewood, Ill.: Dorsey Press, 1962.

Back, Kurt. *Beyond Words.* New York: Russell Sage Foundation, 1972.

Baldridge, J. Victor. *Power and Conflict in the University.* New York: John Wiley & Sons, 1971.

Bales, Robert F. "Task Roles and Social Roles in Decision-making Groups." In Leonard D. White, ed., *The State of the Social Sciences.* Chicago: The University of Chicago Press, 1956.

Barnard, Chester I. *The Functions of the Executive.* Cambridge, Mass.: Harvard University Press, 1938.

Bauer, Raymond A., ed. *Social Indicators.* Cambridge, Mass.: MIT Press, 1966.

Becker, H. S., ed. *The Other Side.* NewYork: The Free Press, 1964.

Beckhard, Richard. *Organization Development: Strategies and Models.* Reading, Mass.: Addison-Wesley Publishing Company, 1969.

Bendix, Reinhard. *Max Weber: An Intellectual Portrait.* Garden City, New York: Doubleday & Company, 1960.

Bennis, Warren. *Changing Organizations.* New York: McGraw-Hill Book Company, 1966.

Bennis. Warren. *Organization Development.* Reading, Mass.: Addison-Wesley Publishing Company, 1969.

Bennis, Warren G. "A Funny Thing Happened on the Way to the Future." *American Psychologist*, vol. 25 (1970), pp. 595–608.

Bettelheim, Bruno. *Children of the Dream.* New York: The Macmillan Company, 1969.

Black, Max, ed. *Social Theories of Talcott Parsons.* Englewood Cliffs, N. J.: Prentice-Hall, 1961.

Blake, Robert R., and Jane Srygley Mouton. *Building a Dynamic Organization Through Grid Organizational Development.* Reading, Mass.: Addison-Wesley Publishing Company, 1969.

Blau, Peter M. *The Dynamics of Bureaucracy.* Chicago: The University of Chicago Press, 1955.

Blau, Peter M., and W. Richard Scott. *Formal Organizations.* San Francisco: Chandler Publishing Company, 1962.

Blondel, Jean. "Local Government and Local Offices of Ministries in a French Department." *Public Administration,* vol. 37 (1959).

Borgatta, E. F., R. F. Bales, and A. S. Couch. "Some Findings Relevant to the Great Man Theory of Leadership." *American Sociological Review,* vol. 19 (1954), pp. 755–59.

Bradford, Leland, Jack R. Gibb, and Kenneth D. Benne, eds. *T-Group Theory and Laboratory Method.* New York: John Wiley & Sons, 1964.

Braibanti, Ralph ed. *Asian Bureaucratic Systems Emergent from the British Imperial Tradition.* Durham, N. C.: Duke University Press, 1966.

Braybrooke, David, and Charles E. Lindblom. *A Strategy of Decision.* New York: The Free Press of Glencoe, 1963.

Brayfield, Arthur H., and Walter H. Crockett. "Employee Attitudes and Employee Performance." *Psychological Bulletin,* vol. 52 (1955), pp. 396–424.

Bright, James R. *Automation and Management.* Cambridge, Mass.: Graduate School of Business Administration, Harvard University, 1958.

Broder, David S. "The Press: Opposition by Fiat." A column from Washington. *Chicago Sun-Times.* July 7, 1974.

Brown, David S. "Strategies and Tactics of Public Administration Technical Assistance: 1945–1963." In John D. Montgomery and William J. Siffin, eds., *Approaches to Development: Politics, Administration and Change.* New York: McGraw-Hill Book Company, 1966.

Buchanan, Paul C. "Laboratory Training and Organization Development," *Administrative Science Quarterly,* vol. 14 (September, 1969), pp. 466–77.

Bureau of Economic Research. *The Rate and Direction of Inventive Activities.* Princeton, N. J.: Princeton University Press, 1962.

Burns, Tom, and B. M. Stalker. *The Management of Innovations.* London: Tavistock Publications, 1959.

Campbell, John P., and Marvin D. Dunnette. "Effectiveness of T-Group Experiences in Managerial Training and Development." *Psychological Bulletin,* vol. 70 (1968).

Carlson, Richard J., ed. *University of Illinois Assembly on the Ombudsman.* Urbana, Ill.: University of Illinois Institute of Government and Public Affairs, 1969.

Cartwright, Dorwin, and Alvin Zander, eds. *Group Dynamics,* 3rd ed. New York: Harper & Row, 1968.

Carver, Fred D., and Thomas J. Sergiovanni, eds. *Organizations and Human Behavior: Focus on Schools.* New York: McGraw-Hill Book Company, 1969.

Chapman, Brian. *The Prefects and Provincial France.* London: Allen & Unwin, 1955.

Chapman, Brian. *The Profession of Government.* London: Unwin University Books, 1959.

Clausen, J. A., ed. *Socialization and Society.* Boston: Little, Brown & Company, 1968.

Collier, Donald W. "An Innovation System for the Larger Company." *Research Management* (September 1970), pp. 341–48.

Dahl, Robert A., and Charles E. Lindblom. *Politics, Economics and Welfare.* New York: Harper & Brothers, 1953.

Dahrendorf, Ralph. *Class and Class Conflict in Industrial Society.* Stanford, Calif.: Stanford University Press, 1959.

Dale, H. E. *The Higher Civil Service of Great Britain.* London: Oxford University Press, 1941.

Derthick, Martha. *Between State and Nation: Regional Organizations of the United States.* Washington, D.C.: The Brookings Institution, 1974.

Dorn, Dean S., and Gary L. Long. "Sociology and the Radical Right: A Critical Analysis." *The American Sociologist,* vol. 7 (1972).

Downs, Anthony. *Inside Bureaucracy.* Boston: Little, Brown & Company, 1967.

Drucker, Peter F. *The Age of Discontinuity.* New York: Harper & Row, 1969.

Durkheim, Emile. *Suicide,* translated by John A. Spauldine and George Simpson. Glencoe, Ill.: The Free Press, 1951.

Durkheim, Emile. *The Divisions of Labor in Society.* Translated by George Simpson. New York: The Macmillan Company, 1933.

du Sautoy, Peter. *The Civil Service.* London: Oxford University Press, 1957.

English, Gary. "The Trouble with Community Action." *Public Administration Review,* vol. 32 (May-June 1972), pp. 224–31.

Etzioni, Amatai. *The Comparative Analysis of Complex Organizations.* New York: The Free Press, 1961.

Fallers, Lloyd A. *Bantu Bureaucracy.* London: W. Heffer & Sons, n.d.

Ferkiss, Victor C. "The Role of the Public Services in Nigeria and Ghana." In Ferrel Heady and Sybil L. Stokes, eds., *Papers in Comparative Administration.* Ann Arbor, Mich.: Institute of Public Administration, University of Michigan, 1962.

Fesler, James W. "The Political Role of Field Administration." In Ferrel Heady and Sybil L. Stokes, eds., *Papers in Comparative Public Administration.* Ann Arbor, Mich.: Institute of Public Administration, University of Michigan, 1962.

Fleishman, E. A. "Leadership Climate, Human Relations Training, and Supervisory Behavior." *Personnel Psychology,* vol. 6 (1953), pp. 205–22.

Fried, Robert C. *The Italian Prefects: A Study in Administrative Politics.* New Haven, Conn.: Yale University Press, 1963.

Geiger, Kurt. "Changing Political Attitudes in Totalitarian Society: A Case Study of the Role of the Family." *World Politics,* vol. 8 (January, 1956), pp. 187–205.

Gellhorn, Walter. *When Americans Complain.* Cambridge, Mass.: Harvard University Press, 1966.

Gerwig, Robert, and Wilson Freeman. "The Art of Military Ombudsmanship." In L. Harold Levinson, ed., *Our Kind of Ombudsman.* Studies in Public Administration No. 32, Public Administration Clearing Service, University of Florida, 1970.

Gilfillan, S. C. *The Sociology of Invention.* Federalsburg, Md.: Stowell, 1935.

Gladden, E. N. *The Civil Service: Its Problems and Future.* London: Staples Press Limited, 1945.

Goffman, Erving. *Asylums.* Chicago: Aldine Publishing Company, 1962.

Goffman, Erving. *The Presentation of Self in Everyday Life.* Garden City, N. Y.: Doubleday & Company, 1959.

Golden, E. H. "Literary and Social Change in Underdeveloped Countries." *Rural Sociology,* vol. 20 (1955), pp. 1–7.

Golembiewski, Robert T. *Renewing Organizations.* Itaska, Ill.: F. E. Peacock Publishers, 1972.

Goodnow, Frank. *Politics and Administration.* New York: The Macmillan Company, 1900.

Goslin, D. A., ed. *Handbook of Socialization Theory and Research.* Chicago, Ill.: Rand McNally & Company, 1969.

Gouldner, Alvin W. "Red Tape as a Social Problem." In Robert K. Merton, *et al.,* eds., *Reader in Bureaucracy.* Glencoe, Ill.: The Free Press, 1952.

Gouldner, Alvin W. "Organizational Analysis." In Robert K. Merton, *et al., Sociology Today.* New York: Basic Books, 1959.

Greenberg, Martin H. *Bureaucracy and Development: A Mexican Case Study.* Lexington, Mass.: D. C. Heath & Co., 1970.

Greenstein, Fred I. *The Ameircan Party System and the American People.* Englewood Cliffs, N. J.: Prentice-Hall, 1964.

Guetzkow, Harold, Garley A. Forehand, and Bernard J. James. "An Evaluation of Educational Influence on Administrative Judgment." *Administrative Science Quarterly,* vol. 6 (1961-62), pp. 483–500.

Gulick, John. "Conservatism and Change in a Lebonese Village." *Middle East Journal,* vol. 8 (Summer, 1954), pp. 295–307.

Gulick, Luther. "Notes on the Theory of Organization." In Luther Gulick and Lyndall F. Urwick, eds., *Papers on the Science of Administration.* New York: Institute of Public Administration, 1937.

Guyot, James F. "Bureaucratic Transformations in Burma." In Ralph Braibanti, ed., *Asian Bureaucratic Systems Emergent from the British Imperial Tradition.* Durham, N. C.: Duke University Press, 1966.

Himmelfarb, Milton, and Nathan Glazer. "McGovern and the Jews: A Debate." *Commentary,* vol. 54 (September, 1972), pp. 43–51.

Hlavacek, James D., and Victor A. Thompson. "Bureaucracy and New Product Innovation." *Academy of Management Journal,* vol. 16 (September, 1973), pp. 361–72.

Homans, George. *The Human Group.* New York: Harcourt Brace & World, 1950.

Hook, Sidney. "The Rights of the Victims." *Encounter,* vol. 38 (April, 1972), pp. 11–15.

House, Robert J. "T-Group Education and Leadership Effectiveness: A Review of the Empirical Literature and a Critical Evaluation." *Personnel Psychology,* vol. 20 (Spring, 1967).

House, Robert J., and Lawrence A. Wigdor. "Herzberg's Dual-Factor Theory of Job Satisfaction and Motivation: A Review of the Evidence and a Criticism." *Personnel Psychology,* vol. 20 (1967), pp. 369–89.

Howton, William. *Functionaries.* Chicago: Quadrangle Books, 1969.

Hulin, Charles L. and Milton R. Blood. "Job Enlargement, Individual Differences, and Worker Responses." *Psychological Bulletin,* vol. 69 (1968), pp. 41–55.

Huntington, Samuel P. "Interservice Competition and the Roles of the Armed Services." *American Political Science Review,* vol. 55 (March, 1961), pp. 40–52.

Huntington, Samuel P. "Congressional Responses to the Twentieth Century." In David Truman, ed., *The Congress and America's Future*. Englewood Cliffs, N. J.: Prentice-Hall, 1965.

Huntington, Samuel P. *Political Order in Changing Societies*. New Haven, Conn.: Yale University Press, 1968.

Huntington, Samuel P. "Postindustrial Politics: How Benign Will It Be?" *Comparative Politics*, vol. 6 (1974), pp. 163–91.

Hyden, Goren. *Political Developmen tin Rural Tanzania*. Nairobi, Kenya: East African Publishing House, 1969.

Inglehart, Ronald. "The Silent Revolution in Europe: Intergenerational Change in Post-Industrial Society." *American Political Science Review*, vol. 65 (December, 1971), pp. 991–1017.

Jahoda, Marie. *Current Concepts of Positive Mental Health*. New York: Basic Books, 1958.

Kahn, Robert L., *et al. Organizational Stress*. New York: John Wiley & Sons, 1964.

Kammerer, Gladys M., and John M. DeGrove. *Florida City Managers*. Studies in Public Administration No. 22, Gainesville, Fla.: Public Administration Clearing Service, University of Florida, 1961.

Kaufman, Herbert. "Administrative Decentralization and Political Power." In Francis Rourke, ed., *Bureaucratic Power in National Politics*, 2nd ed. Boston: Little, Brown & Company, 1972.

Kay, Hubert. "Harnessing the R. and D. Monster." *Fortune*, January, 1965, at p. 160.

Kerr, Clark, John T. Dunlop, Frederick Harbison and Charles A. Myers. *Industrialism and Industrial Man*. New York: Oxford University Press, 1964.

Kingsley, J. Donald. "Bureaucracy and Political Development, with Particular Reference to Nigeria." In Joseph LaPalombara, ed., *Bureaucracy and Political Development*. Princeton, N. J.: The Princeton University Press, 1963.

Laing, R. D. *The Politics of the Family and Other Essays*. New York: Pantheon Books, 1971.

Lambert, H. E. *Kikuyu Social and Political Institutions*. London: Oxford University Press, 1956.

Landau, Martin. "Redundancy, Rationality, and the Problem of Duplication and Overlap." *Public Administration Review*, vol. 29 (July-August 1969), pp. 346–58.

LaPalombara, Joseph, ed. *Bureaucracy and Poliitcal Development*. Princeton, N. J.: The Princeton University Press, 1963.

Lawler, Edward E., III, and Lyman W. Porter. "The Effect of Performance on Job Satisfaction." *Industrial Relations*, vol. 7 (October, 1967), pp. 20–28.

Lawrence, Paul R., and Jay W. Lorsch. *Developing Organizations*. Reading, Mass.: Addison-Wesley Publishing Company, 1969.

Leavitt, H. J. "Unhealthy Organizations." In H. J. Leavitt and L. Pondy, eds., *Readings in Managerial Psychology*. Chicago: The University of Chicago Press, 1964.

Lemert, E. M. *Human Deviance, Social Problems and Social Control*. Englewood Cliffs, N. J.: Prentice-Hall, 1967.

Lerner, Daniel. *The Passing of Traditional Society*. Glencoe, Ill.: The Free Press, 1958.

Lerner, Daniel. "Towards a Communication Theory of Modernization." In Lucien W. Pye, ed., *Communications and Political Development*. Princeton, N. J.: The Princeton University Press, 1963.

Levitt, Theodore. *The Marketing Mode: Pathways to Corporate Growth.* New York: McGraw-Hill Book Company, 1970.

Levinson, Harold L., ed. *Our Kind of Ombudsman.* Studies in Public Administration No. 32, Public Administration Clearing Service, University of Florida, 1970.

Levy, Marion J., Jr. *The Structure of Society.* Princeton, N. J.: The Princeton University Press, 1952.

Levy-Bruhl, Lucien. *Primitive Mentality.* Boston: Beacon Press, 1966.

Likert, Rensis. *The Human Organization: Its Management and Value.* New York: McGraw-Hill Book Company, 1967.

Lindblom, Charles E. *The Intelligence of Democracy.* New York: The Free Press, 1965.

Lindblom, Charles E. *The Policy-Making Process.* Englewood Cliffs, N. J.: Prentice-Hall, 1968.

Little, Arthur D., Inc./Industrial Research Institute, Inc. *Barriers to Innovation in Industry: Opportunities for Public Policy Changes.* National Science Foundation, Contracts NSF-C748 and C725, 1973.

Lorch, Barbara R. "Reverse Discrimination in Hiring in Sociology Departments: A Preliminary Report." *The American Sociologist,* vol. 8 (August, 1973), pp. 116–20.

Lorsch, Jay W. *Product Innovation and Organization.* New York: The Macmillan Company, 1965.

Lowi, Theodore J. *The End of Liberalism.* New York: W. W. Norton & Company, 1969.

Lyden, Fremont J., and Ernest G. Miller, eds. *Planning Programming Budgeting: A Systems Approach to Management.* Chicago: Markham Publishing Company, 1967.

Macridis, Roy C. "France." In Roy C. Macridis and Robert E. Ward, eds., *Modern Political Systems: Europe.* Englewood Cliffs, N. J.: Prentice-Hall, 1968.

Mainzer, Lewis C. *Political Bureaucracy.* Glenview, Ill.: Scott, Foresman & Company, 1973.

Malcolm, Donald G., and Alan J. Rowe, eds. *Management Control Systems.* New York: John Wiley & Sons, 1960.

Mannheim, Karl. *Ideology and Utopia.* New York: Harcourt, Brace & Company, 1936.

March, James G., and Herbert A. Simon. *Organizations.* New York: John Wiley & Sons, 1958.

Marcson, Simon. *The Scientist in American Industry.* Princeton, N. J.: Industrial Relations School, 1960.

Marini, Frank, ed. *Toward a New Public Administration.* Scranton, Pa.: Chandler Publishing Company, 1971.

Maslow, A. H. *Motivation and Personality.* New York: Harper & Brothers, 1954.

McGuire, Joseph W. "The Collegiate Business School Today." *Collegiate News and Notes,* vol. 25 (Spring, 1972), pp. 1–5.

Merton, Robert K. "Bureaucratic Structure and Personality." *Social Forces,* vol. 17 (1940), pp. 560–68.

Merton, Robert K. *Social Theory and Social Structure.* Glencoe, Ill.: The Free Press, 1957.

Merton, Robert K., et al., eds. *Reader in Bureaucracy.* Glencoe, Ill.: The Free Press, 1952.

Merton, Robert K., and Paul Lazersfeld, eds. *Continuities in Social Research: Studies in the Scope and Method of "The American Soldier".* Glencoe, Ill.: The Free Press, 1950.

Metzger, Bert L., and Jerome A. Colletti. *Does Profit Sharing Pay?* Evanston, Ill.: Profit Sharing Research Foundation, 1971.

Miller, Daniel R., and Guy E. Swanson. *The Changing American Parent.* New York: John Wiley & Sons, 1958.

Miner, John B. "Changes in Student Attitudes Toward Bureaucratic Role Prescriptions During the 1960's." *Administrative Science Quarterly,* vol. 16 (September, 1971), pp. 351–64.

Mogulof, Melvin B. "Federal Interagency Action and Inaction: The Federal Regional Council Experience." *Public Administration Review,* vol. 32 (May-June 1972), pp. 232–40.

Moore, Wilbert E., and Arnold S. Feldman. *Labor Commitment and Social Change in Developing Areas.* New York: Social Science Research Council, 1960.

Moynihan, Daniel P. "Income by Right." *The New Yorker,* January 13, 20, and 27, 1973.

Nader, Ralph, *et al.,* eds. *Whistle Blowing.* New York: Grossman Publishers, 1972.

Nelson, Richard R. "The Economics of Invention: A Survey of the Literature." *Journal of Business,* vol. 32 (April, 1959), p. 114.

Neustadt, Richard E. "Politicians and Bureaucrats." In David Truman, ed., *The Congress and America's Future.* Englewood Cliffs, N. J.: Prentice-Hall, 1965.

Niskanen, William, Jr. *Bureaucracy and Representative Government.* Chicago: Aldine-Atherton Publishing Co., 1971.

Novak, Michael. *The Rise of the Unmeltable Ethnics.* New York: The Macmillan Company, 1971.

Novick, David. *Program Budgeting.* Washington, D.C.: Government Printing Office, 1965.

Oakeshott, Michael. *Rationalism in Politics and Other Essays.* New York: Basic Books Publishing Co., 1962.

Odiorne, G. S. "The Trouble with Sensitivity Training." *Training and Development Journal,* vol. 17 (October, 1963).

Parsons, Talcott. *The Social System.* Glencoe, Ill.: The Free Press, 1951.

Parsons, Talcott. *Structure and Process in Modern Society.* Glencoe, Ill.: The Free Press, 1960.

Parsons, Talcott. "Pattern Variables Revisited." *American Sociological Review,* vol. 25 (August, 1960), pp. 467–83.

Parsons, Talcott, Robert F. Bales, and Edward A. Shills. *Working Papers in The Theory of Action.* Glencoe, Ill.: The Free Press, 1953.

Parsons, Talcott, and Edward A. Shills, eds. *Toward a General Theory of Action.* Cambridge, Mass.: Harvard University Press, 1959.

Patai, Raphael. "The Dynamics of Westernization in the Middle East." *Middle East Journal,* vol. 9 (Winter, 1955), pp. 1–16.

Pelz, Donald C. and Frank M. Andrews. *Scientists in Organizations: Productive Climates for Research and Development.* New York: John Wiley & Sons, 1966.

Piven, Francis Fox. "Militant Civil Servants in New York City." *Transaction,* vol. 7 (November, 1969), pp. 24–28, 55.

Presthus, Robert V. *The Organizational Society.* New York: Alfred A. Knopf, 1962.

Price, Don. *Government and Science.* New York: New York University Press, 1954.

Rand, Ayn. *We the Living.* New York: The New American Library, 1959.

Reynolds, William G. "The Executive Synecdoche." *Business Topics* (Autumn, 1969), pp. 21–29.

Riedel, James A. "Citizen Participation: Myths and Realities." *Public Administration Review,* vol. 32 (May-June 1972), pp. 211–20.

Riesman, David, Nathan Glazer, and Reuel Denney. *The Lonely Crowd.* Garden City, New Jersey: Doubleday & Company, 1953.

Riggs, Fred W. "Agraria and Industria—Towards a Typology of Comparative Administration." In William J. Siffin, ed., *Toward the Comparative Study of Administration.* Bloomington, Ind.: Indiana University Press, 1957.

Riggs, Fred W. *Administration in Developing Countries.* Boston: Houghton Mifflin Company, 1964.

Riggs, Fred W. *Thailand: The Modernization of a Bureaucratic Polity.* Honolulu: East-West Center Press, 1966.

Riggs, Fred W. "The Sala Model: An Ecological Approach to the Study of Comparative Administration.' 'In Nimrod Raphaeli, ed., *Readings in Comparative Administration.* Boston: Allyn & Bacon, 1967.

Rogers, David. *110 Livingston Street.* New York: Random House, 1968.

Rourke, Francis E. *Bureaucratic Power in National Politics,* 2nd ed. Boston: Little, Brown & Company, 1972.

Saltanoff, Louis. "The Innovation Myth." *Industrial Research* (August, 1971), pp. 45–46.

Sarbin, Theodore R. "Role Theory." In Gardner Lindzey, ed., *Handbook of Social Psychology,* vol. I. Cambridge, Mass.: Addison-Wesley Publishing Company, 1954.

Sartori, Giovanni. "European Political Parties: The Case of Polarized Pluralism." In Joseph LaPalombara and Myron Wiener, eds., *Political Parties and Political Development.* Princeton, N. J.: The Princeton University Press, 1966.

Schein, Edgar H. "Forces Which Undermine Managerial Development." *California Managerial Review,* vol. 5 (Summer, 1963), pp. 23–34.

Schick, Allen. *Budget Innovation in the States.* Washington, D.C.: The Brookings Institution, 1971.

Schick, Allen. "A Death in the Bureaucracy." *Public Administration Review,* vol. 33 (March-April, 1973), pp. 146–56.

Schulman, Sam. "Basic Functional Roles in Nursing: Mother Surrogate and Healer." In E. Gartly Jaco, ed., *Patients, Physicians and Illness.* Glencoe, Ill.: The Free Press, 1958.

Selznick, Philip. *Leadership in Administration.* Evanston, Ill.: Row, Peterson & Company, 1957.

Shepard, Herbert A. "The T-Group as Training in Observant Participation." In Warren G. Bennis, Kenneth D. Benne, and Robert Chin, eds., *The Planning of Change.* New York: Holt, Rinehart & Winston, 1962.

Shepard, Herbert A. "Changing Interpersonal and Intergroup Relationships in Organizations." In James G. March, ed., *Handbook of Organizations.* Chicago: Rand McNally & Company, 1965.

Shonfield, Andrew. *Modern Capitalism.* London: Oxford University Press, 1965.

Shutz, Alfred. *The Phenomenology of the Social World.* Translated by George Walsh and Frederick Lehnert. Evanston, Ill.: Northwestern University Press, 1967.

Simon, Herbert A. *Adminsitrative Behavior.* New York: The Macmillan Company, 1947.

Simon, Herbert A., Donald W. Smithburg, and Victor A. Thompson. *Public Administration.* New York: Alfred A. Knopf, 1950.

Sjoberg, Gideon, Richard A. Bryner, and Buford Farris. "Bureaucracy and the Lower Class." *Sociology and Social Research,* vol. 50 (April, 1966), pp. 325–37.

Skinner, B. F. *Beyond Freedom and Dignity.* New York: Alfred A. Knopf, 1971.

Smith, Adam. *The Wealth of Nations.* 1776.

Snow, C. P. *Science and Government.* New York: Mentor Books, 1962.

Solzhenitsyn, Alexander. *One Day in the Life of Ivan Denisovich.* New York: Praeger Publishers, 1963.

Solzhenitsyn, Alexander. *Gulag Archipelago.* New York: Harper & Row, 1974.

Spaeth, Harold J. *An Introduction to Supreme Court Decision Making.* San Francisco: Chandler Publishing Company, 1965.

Stauffer, Samuel, *et al. The American Soldier,* vol. I. Princeton, N. J.: The Princeton University Press, 1949.

Stein, Morris I. and Shirley J. Vidich, eds. *Creativity and the Individual.* Glencoe, Ill.: The Free Press, 1960.

Stein, Morris I., and Shirley J. Vidich. *Survey of Psychological Literature in the Area of Creativity With View Toward Needed Research.* New York: New York University Press, 1962.

Stinchcombe, Arthur L. "Social Structure and Organizations." In James G. March, ed., *Handbook of Organizations.* Chicago: Rand McNally & Company, 1965.

Surlsin, Marvin, and Alan Wolfe, eds. *An End to Political Science: The Caucus Papers.* New York: Basic Books, 1970.

Sykes, A. J. M. "The Effect of a Supervisory Training Course in Changing Supervisor's Perceptions and Expectations of the Role of Management." *Human Relations,* vol. 15 (Summer, 1962), pp. 227–43.

Thomas, Donald W., and Jean Mayer. "The Search for the Secret of Fat." *Psychology Today,* vol. 7 (September, 1973), p. 74.

Thompson, Victor A. *The Regulatory Process in OPA Rationing.* New York: Kings Crown Press, 1950.

Thompson, Victor A. *Modern Organization.* New York: Alfred A. Knopf, 1961.

Thompson, Victor A. *Bureaucracy and Innovation.* University, Ala.: The University of Alabama Press, 1969.

Thompson, Victor A. *Decision Theory, Pure and Applied.* Morristown, N. J.: General Learning Press, 1971.

Thompson, Victor A. *Organizations as Systems.* Morristown, N. J.: General Learning Press, 1973.

Thompson, Victor A. *The Development of Modern Organization: Tools Out of People.* Morristown, N. J.: General Learning Press, 1974.

Thompson, Victor A. *Bureaucracy and Innovative Action.* Morristown, N. J.: General Learning Press, 1975.

Toffler, Alvin. *Future Shock.* New York: Random House, 1970.

Townsend, Robert. *Up the Organization.* New York: Alfred A. Knopf, 1970.

Tumin, Melvin M. "Some Dysfunctions of Institutional Imbalances." *Behavioral Science,* vol. I (July, 1956), pp. 218–23.

Waldo, Dwight, ed. *Public Administration in a Time of Turbulence.* Scranton, Pa.: Chandler Publishing Company, 1971.

Weber, Max. *The Theory of Social and Economic Organizaiton.* Translated by A. M. Henderson and Talcott Parsons. New York: Oxford University Press, 1947.

Westin, Allen F. *Privacy and Freedom.* New York: Atheneum Publishers, 1967.

Whisler, Thomas L. *Executives and Their Jobs—The Changing Organizational Structure.* Selected Papers No. 9, Graduate School of Business, University of Chicago, 1964.

Whyte, William H., Jr. *The Organization Man.* Garden City, N. Y.: Doubleday and Co., 1957.

Wildavsky, Aaron. *The Politics of the Budgetary Process.* Boston: Little, Brown & Company, 1964.

Wildavsky, Aaron. "The Self-Evaluating Organization." *Public Administration Review,* vol. 32 (September-October, 1972), pp. 509–20.

Wilson, Francis G. *The Elements of Modern Politics.* New York: McGraw-Hill Book Company, 1936.

Wilson, Woodrow. "The Study of Administration." *Political Science Quarterly,* vol. 2 (1887), pp. 197–222.

Wittfogel, Karl A. *Oriental Despotism.* New Haven, Conn.: Yale University Press, 1957.

Wolfe, Julie C., Melvin L. DeFleur, and Walter L. Slocum. "Sex Discrimination in Hiring Practices of Graduate Sociology Departments: Myths and Realities." *The American Sociologist,* vol. 8 (November, 1973), pp. 159–65.

Wraith, Ronald and Edgar Simpkins. *Corruption in Developing Countries.* New York: W. W. Norton & Company, 1964.

Wurfel, David. "Foreign Aid and Social Reform in Political Development: A Philippine Case Study." *American Political Science Review,* vol. 53 (June, 1959), pp. 456–82.

Zimmerman, Joseph F. "Neighborhoods and Citizen Involvement." *Public Administration Review,* vol. 32 (May-June), pp. 201–10.

Index

Golden rule, 90, 91
Good looks, 74
Governor, 49, 50, 55, 56
Graft, 88
Griffiths, Representative Martha, 85
Guyana, 75

Harmony, 25, 30
Hawaii, 62
Health, organization, 24, 27
Health, Education and Welfare, Department of (HEW), 56, 61, 77, 78
HEW guidelines, 78
Healthy organizations, 25, 26
Height, minimum, 75, 76
Hicks, Eleanor, 77
Hierarchy, 34, 93, 94
Hitler, 73
Homeostatic processes, 15, 16, 35
Hospital, 21
Howton, William, 14
Human-relations training, 31
Huntington, Samuel P., 34

Illinois, 73
Impersonal: action, 4, 9, 17; organization, 18, 21; relations, 13, 67; treatment, 19, 40, 66
Impersonality, 32, 33, 34, 38, 40, 51, 58, 59, 60, 62, 65, 88, 91
Incarceration in mental institutions, 28
India, 46
Indiana, 74
India-Pakistan war, 46
Industrial worker, 5
Industrialism, 5, 6, 41
Inequality, 13, 83, 84
In loco parentis, 22
Inmates, 41, 64, 67
Innovation, 15, 93, 96
Inspector General, 63
Institutionalization, 44
Instrumental problems, 48
Insurance, national health, 86
Integration, 69
Interpersonal skills, 27
Interservice commands, 35
Inversion of means and ends, 1
Ireland, 46
Irrationality, 25, 32

Israel, 39, 46, 92
Italy, 49, 53, 54, 78

Jahoda, Marie, 24
Japan, 62
Jews, 77, 78
Johnson, President Lyndon B., 95
Joint Economic Committee of Congress, 61
Journalists, 61
Joy in work, 10
Justice of the peace, 12

Kant, 90, 91
Kaufman, Herbert, 55, 57
Kennedy, Senator Edward, 46
Kibbutz, 92
Kinship, 49, 87, 89

Labeling theory, 83
Laboratory training, 26
Landau, Martin, 38
LATER (Left-handed Alliance Toward Equal Rights), 76
Latinos, 56, 57, 71
Lavelle, General, 15
Lawyers, 9, 40, 61, 68, 70
Leaders, 31, 44
League of Women Voters, 72
Legal aid, 20
Legislatures, 56, 57
Legitimacy, 43, 68, 88
Lerner, Daniel, 87
Lettuce boycott, 81, 82
Lie-detector, 39
Life-span perspective, 85–86
Likert, Rensis, 25
Lindsay, Mayor John, 56
Lineage, 49
Little city halls, 56
Lowi, Theodore, 67, 96, 97
Lucknow, India, 97
Ludditism, 32–33

Machine, political, 48, 49, 57
Maintenance: group, 90–91; problems, 48, 51, 52; functions, political, 51, 52, 55
Maladministration, 63, 64
Management Safeguards, Inc., 39
Management science, 24, 95, 96
Mannheim, Karl, 13

Subversion, 11, 25
Suicide, 88
SST (Supersonic Transport), 32
Supreme Soviet, 72, 76, 91
Survival, 15, 16, 26, 31, 35, 44, 46
Sweden, 61, 62, 63
System: artificial, 13, 16, 17, 26, 28, 29, 30, 31, 34, 35, 38, 43, 44, 46, 92 96, 97; natural, 15, 16, 17, 24, 26, 28, 30, 31, 34, 35, 43, 44, 46, 92, 96, 97

Tall people, 73, 84
Task-oriented, 30, 31
Temporary organization, 34, 35, 93
T-Group training, 21, 26–31
Theft, 10, 11, 23, 66, 90
Tools, 9, 10, 13, 17, 23, 25, 26, 43, 44, 60
Total institutions, 41, 64
Training: administrative, 21, 23, 30; sensivity, 26–31; T-Group, 21, 26–31
Tribalism, 18, 29, 49, 87, 89
Truman, Harry, 47
Tutelage, 54
TV commercials, 22

Ulster, 47

Underdeveloped countries, 5, 12, 18, 59
Unions, 7, 46, 47
Unit costs, 41
Universalism, 4, 11, 17, 18, 51
Universalistic norms, 4, 11, 17, 18, 51

Venture group, 36–37
Viceroy, 50, 51, 54
Vietnam: country, 15; War, 81
Virginity, 85
Virgins' Anti-Defamation League, 85

"Wash out" effect of training, 31
Washington, D. C., 77, 95
Waste, 38
Watergate, 47
Weber, Max, 9, 13, 36
Welfare, 10, 11
Wisconsin, 74
Wizard of Oz, 47
Women's Bureau, 92
Women's liberation, 66, 92
World War II, 51

Ximenes, Vincent T., 75

Zero redundancy, 38